Wrack Lariat

Heller Levinson

BLACK
WIDOW
PRESS

Boston, MA

Wrack Lariat

Black Widow Press is an imprint of Commonwealth Books, Inc., Boston, MA. Distributed to the trade by NBN (National Book Network) throughout North America, Canada, and the U.K. All Black Widow Press books are printed on acid-free paper, and glued into bindings. Black Widow Press and its logo are registered trademarks of Commonwealth Books, Inc.

Joseph S. Phillips and Susan J. Wood, Ph.D., Publishers
www.blackwidowpress.com

Design & production: Kerrie Kemperman

Cover art and title pages: *Bone Springs Rain Grass,* detail, 2005, by Linda Lynch

Other Illustrations:
PowPoi #7 and #11 by Kurt Devrese in "The Dot Soliloquies"
Lines, I; Lines, II; Lines, III; Large Empty Drawing; Empty Drawing, I; Empty Drawing, II; Empty Drawing, III; From the Velocity; and *Lilt* by Linda Lynch in "Linda Lynch"

ISBN-13: 978-0-9960079-8-6

Printed in the United States
10 9 8 7 6 5 4 3 2 1

for Mary,
for Manitou

"Nay, nor the unmatched phoenix lives anew,
Unless she burn."

Michelangelo, from Sonnet 59

MODULES

How much of /

w

H

o

O

s   h

"Objects in motion multiply and distort themselves
like vibrations
passing through space."

—from the "Futurist Manifesto," 1912.

how much of hinges

The "how much of" modules developed to densify the particle (the subject matter). As they cropped up in various applications, I noted their luminous nature when stood-apart, highlit by their own provocations.

I considered how much of "how much of's" appeal was due to its traditional usage as a quantitative query, now reoriented to release metaphysical posits.

In this Hinge Capacity, "how much of" moves toward *consideration* rather than *conclusion*.

wHoosh Hinge Cogitation

wHoosh is the first Module to exfoliate applications through evocation rather than contextual gristle. Former modules shaped (tossed) particles into contour by means of a specific pivot, i.e., "smelling," "with," "the road to ___ road," etc.

wHoosh activates particles by means of Meteoric Velocity, the sheer gaseous turbulence producing wakes of manifestation.

This galactic linguistic storm can also shift the nature of the particle from a one-worded subject, such as "plangency" or "mermaid," to multi-worded, multi-lined Nuclear Spray.

how much of

evanescence

is

acquittal

wHoosh

◻

bushwhack craven carve legerdemain circumstantial mole the
bred upon lost in the lily pond curtailment schoolyard no longer
refuse but refusal the rebuttal a butt buttressing stampede
conformity outlandish socks the telltale sign how you dress for
how you walk if you don't walk you aren't going anywhere this
is no more a discovery than a séance with hiccups where are you
when we need you Mr. Phillips don't answer that its disquiet
distemper a template of meridional scorch medicinal stench
countercultural subterfuge folk song bucket lamentation mesas
seldom left behind skid marks path the road to lachrymose road
smelling novelty smelling rent pavement wheelin' hell bent
dissatisfactions down at the factory enter here
smart parts delineate a reckoning leftovers soon stink
skank &
the wilderness
experience

how much of

elasticity

                         is

earned

◻

studying the history of the repeat sign :‖ leads to assessing time
as an event uncomfortable with registration the way pageantry
disguises the lisp or a lipover improves the tongue without
regard to improving performance laboratories crunch
cannibalistic back-door recursions nadiral intoxications
in the cardinality of bridge compresses the long syllabic bias

how much of

rambunction

is

plea

◻

pony-up pullulative rake bastion fever frills
forensic quill
fructuous cake
archering ponytail hagiographic centrifuge
how many ways to count a thing
the belly
bellicose
banjo

how much of

ecumenical

is

persuasion

◻

a calliope calypso
collisions incontrovertible
incontestability unaccountable
breeze tongue wing booze
cakey collateral conch conk crenellate casket basket cinch-wrap
rimroar
pearlized circumstantial slut

how much of

her back

would write

epics

¤

forever is not not that it is not
trip-worthy just that it is a lapse
overlooking governable non-compliance
yet earnest

upon these shores momentum grows
seemly
at times, gorgeous

how much of

love

    is

        apparition

how much of

love

is

moisture

◻

                                                        abeyance
arbitration douses dosage a love song conveyor conveyoring
upshot upstart cistern considering explore deplore powerlines
blot intestinal inflammation cavort distribution systems signal
ethics committee the state of harridan overwhelm fracas in the
engine room undermine rhymetime serpentine sinuous ://:
sensuous in twists & turns eros turnstiles unabetted unabate call
it quits or catch it on the fly
fracas in the engine room
get a clue   take a ticket
get
on
line

how much of

commotion is

arrangement

misconstrued

missteps

aligning

◻

wallop bushwhack marathon galaxy gong maintenance
misdemeanor prayer session workshops crux conga slap
meander larynx swell, elbow grease, crow's feet, elaborative
bunions sloop IOUs health ripe lettuce river rapids
    incremental would be disturbing were it not for the
abundancy of truancy wards, avocado trusts, boat slips, I am no
longer clear about manifestos, I am no longer
clear

how much of

earth-cunning

is

dig

◻

sword forged from cloud   scraping the deer's
hind   jettisoning lumber
sword of the thousand lungs
blade of febrile nipples
rain-peeler
glyph-slayer
tambourine-hacker
slashing savagery, thirst
earth-cunning   forest-conniver
fathom heaver
weep lode ladling phantom longings skirt sanctity steamship
seminars
mercurial paste
sword of wood of wheat of oath   skirl-dancer
sh(r)ed sh(r)ill seafarer crib crossover cuneiform drills
cavalry
linseed
rabble slicer rouse quell rubric rostrum nostrum detonator
absalom solution
absolution severely esteemed caretaker blood
legislator legislation
heft
hoist

how much of

stillness

races through motion

◻

eruption commotion combustion →
plumb
zone tone
tomb tumbling tome tunnel runes
rambunctions
knee/kneecaps articulating
obsidian keyboard caul
hawkwings bodiless winging
air-welders
smith-bakers
seas
unwrinkling

how much of

consanguinity

is

seed(ing)

◻

triply accumulative → snow frost solar flares hair
climactically reactionary hoary reflex late Saurian disorder a
condition never fairly hardly ever compensatory during combat
the load the loan loin the lurch purloined in exquisite acquisition
with rewards the watermelon man jauntyjoggering capsules the
candy store petty thievery coggery lynch pillory bugger quarter
dismissed searchlight for foot the lost diagonal *Have*
we a right to assume the survival of something that was
originally there, alongside of what was later derived from it? the
chieftain & the pirate settling upon an appropriate ceremonial
chiseling rare craftsmanship jointure psalms jubilating spore-
flurries-fuselage
clairvoyance
through
nose

how much of

coterminous

is

consanguinity

◻

toothpick

the purities only extend so far even on the clearest of days there
are voluptuosities beyond reason impurities that could amount
to something were they not deemed counterfeit down at the
surfeit machine wounds plushy pussovered sleek hallmark
hallway hedonism recruitments are up Indianapolis germ
warfare robust stalwart sailing uncomfortable seas warped for
convertibility indecision wavers confronted by gunshot remedial
attempts welcome they call me an eccentric man I don't believe I
am you can get there if you choose

how much of

tongue

is

flappable

◻

    well-nigh erstwhile the dupery foreclosing on glut – glot
glottal – guilt careers the tongue no cause for no problem when
Everything problematic gain gleefully the got counterfeited in a
refuse bin no sin squealing recognition boot to the shin equal
distribution shoe-in glorious shore lineswore confining
splattering smut shoulder smolder smother burble the tube
tuberousness malignant to download an afternoon affair rhino
charming alarming the wilderness imperils carelessness courts
smile the blacksmithing the smote erstwhile

how much of

pilgrimage

is failure

to embrace where you are

◻

wayward
board chord corded to ward cortex aimlessness alimentation
bedfellows buoying belies accordion accordance gramophone
grievances a comeuppance dives hard the trial churly hourly
wage compensation woos cut-offs carts choruses   warehouses
castaways reclaimed how do you like your coffee Mr. B oh no
George you don't buy dandelions this time of year lost roads
offer
gestation gesture
wildly

how much of

clarity

is

clar-i-fi-ca-tion

how much of

clarity

is

reflectivity

◘

ambi-dex-Terity   loosens locutions tribulation on the road
to a fine dinner party pack in as much silverware as you can
manners mannishly the fifth dimension clarity denied
plateworthy status all those yummy grasshoppers to feed
remorse tails trails a function most Westerners cut off the head
taste is a rambunction caboosed to the trilobite ne'er the matter
to mutter materializations stump the ambiwil(y)ling even
keeping fit a round for cereal demonstrations stand-ins stand-
offs stiff skiff stillwater & aubergine arachnoid complexity culls
the weak perversifies the under-qualified what gives the right to
you you the right to give what   transparencies a form of
recklessness nary the chary caring a remonstrance furtive no
longer

how much of

harborage

is

seaworthy

◻

whereuPon bewildering beguilement supposed identity the unraveling in hurry to the station train might be barbells pumping fuel slippage the filling tanks lachrymose wary overdose cherries this time of wily decorates decorum-istically decorumisms drizzle anachronistic sinisterism late with digits bauble-smirks traditional mannerisms prevail during a drought do you always go around in slippers Mr. R? roughage & earth supreme John don't you know harborage is no longer a natural reaction in this era of populismpupilism the #2 pencil suffices in most instances ratatouille delectable melon seasonal sectional occasional bring
lips
to
fish

how much of

circumstance

is

circumstantial

how much of

circumstance   is

provi   den

ti

ality

◻

extraORDiNARily extracts cover a choice of convicts convictions imprisoned in uniformity garb cloister barbs flutter fuchsia foam lavender orthodontics circuits override trouble in the lowlands loiter girth non-apparently disappearance mistrials posture posthumous morbidity postcard watchers glee-chutes choice juice barons polish cinderellas now blasphemous bedridden with loam with Hardy novels deleted from curricula lamp posts squirmy jettison slime eel-cakes flame-riddles gavotte the grasses hymn
risings whorl
mongering

how much of

          melancholy

is longing

for home

◻

oFtentimes the slip skid-skedaddles run amok untucks
thunderstruck deciphering anecdotes a moat bunches piled till
kingdom come comeuppance insubstantially Hal a fair weather
friend until the end that brutal finish code of wheel dubiousness
an enterprise a lurch a mulch for lunch keepsakes on the quick
quirk smirk tremulous with mirth smell embellishes pathfinder
so much about
loneliness

                    &

bathing

how much of

concupiscence

is

arrival

◻

a moat a mi(t)(t)(ght)e a stroke a si(gh)t(e)
tingling delicious — ly — light
ly — gladful glee — ly — grinning matrixes naughtify notary
notify cuirass cunning clarity plates canary cage glean copper
ersatz gleam stepping exercises oblique on the shores of
snoopery mopping in a troubled time detritus & lime dutifully
juice dandelion dust porcine percolative steady in the myth of
ta(i)l(e) trumpery miles thumbs the blue spaniel a blue fin tuna
can sell for over $800,000.00 cogitation a latter day vacuity
sinisterism saddled bedlam in the fracture despair when the hand
fails

how much of

desire
                is
                        fiction,

...

narratives

developing

◻

temporALity muse abuse clues guttural non-promissory fade-in fade-out pearl settings roustabout quicksilver sounding bound liveries bounding gap flushing filtrative mustache pilfer dear credenza show me your drawers

how much of

insight

is domesticated

◻

aPParently a peer a f(l)(lout)aunt a flux f o r m u l a t i n g
contour come to fore a peek a posture a postulate presencing
presen-cing manifestationally announcement prelude pour wisp
mate warble dispatch aperture bore hatch latch loose lark warp
glide pick a path sideways roadside surmise pedicure sunrise spit
spat spot sport spore aC
tually

how much of

drawing

      is

          extrusion

    ....

ferreting from source

how much of

drawing

        is

                intrusion

……………..

source drilling in

◻

oCCASionALly there serves scores sears a severance spot a
spit upon the hill cliff the tempest in repose rune
insubordination & gallimaufry accumulations hardy
preliminaries primarily palimony priorities muff wires pitfall
cheers shears comeuppance galore one takes stock of oneself a
delivery of sorts a parcel inadvertently contagious trespass
chimerae causation calamity parallels I keep tellin' Mike but
Mike don't want to hear it inconsistenciescellophanecarousels
clutch gardens abridgement
abetting troublesome
to get

how much of

art

is

hanging

how much of

hanging

is

display

◻

rarely hardly if ever seldom seen the purview short shorn of
latch crazy with the gravy easy on the mellow driving directions
to your homepage in this time of spite off the light rapiers sleek
silky subtly keen a forage near dear darling of the dank
rapscallion prank opportunities in the buff delectations
deliciously dolorous fold enough's enough huff & puff grab by
the scruff if hardly
if ever

how much of

frostbite

is

warmth lacking

¤

HARdly a moment goes by that I don't think of even the way you kissed me off when I made that minor infraction erring a malcontent displeasure causing febrility slurps rhinoceros teeth cacophonies trash-scraping bins piled high in Majorca pitter-patters frostbite bastion groundlings trouble in the streets vampires vamp the wires speech dysprosody non-representation bewilders the handy preposterous the notion of ambiguity right turns lead to the right

how much of

fucking

        is

                loan

lending oneself

to the other

a lay-a-way

◻

obviousLy there comes a time when satisfaction no longer matters annuls high maintenance derelict benefaction disarray lobes observance peculiarizes the intrinsically insignificant wears upon the bearer peremptory strikers bell toters miniaturized dendrites magnified blunt instruments bone dissipates automatons zippering bland blandishments unworthy putrefying raise a call to leopard skin to paw radicalism tooth uterus skull totem fire twig perch bombinate bizarre landings restorations holying lazing among keyboards bass clarinets notes made of algae

of silt

how much of

music

is fingers

◻

trying to understand why anyone would play the upright bass
lug the heft of bring porting belly full over belt supported
instrument (to be upright, supported) leaning lean to toward
cooperation largeness incline with/to unison warp dance
accept(ing) uplift bring to position alteration skeletal stance
rudiments nutrition tendon bake cumbersome overhaul   hold
tenacity   tenderness   holding hike hug hide a hideaway
holding hides
away
disappearance

how much of

equilibrium

is

distance

◻

if ever there was a cause revolution   sign   intent   deserving
catalyst, frankly speaking forcibly, observe preemptive saintly
sailing on the Thames hermaphrodite suage defocus brume
mood spillovers equations no longer respectable yet recalcitrant
remaking of treaty entreaty testify remaking chicanery knave
poltroon adipostic symbiosis no longer available *painful so
remote*
breaths upon the mist
there is justification

how much of

circumstances beyond our control

is

prophylactic

◻

nevertheless there are circumstances beyond our control
plights   ballistics   barbecues   freestanding marsupials marzipan
ruff with roughage mascara caulked rife with dysentery the very
pigskin calls for an internal investigation artificial sweeteners
support no kid left behind ribbed perilous sustain subsequence
hardly grab the sniff hounds the snorkels the seizures
hagiography habitats under arrest new worlds climatize
breakthroughs in quadratic dynamics resoundingly it's
almost time
for lunch

how much of

mathematics

is

chiseling

how much of

mathematics

is

clinging

◘

nevertheless the preposterous has a way of gaining garnering
gathering given the extremities subsequentialities galore glorify
in underweight in the achievement of molasses spaghetti with
classic marinara sauce sailing at full tide hardly a template to
modify so many concerns alight the brow afflict scowl
parsimony is a declining tautology a life of the mind a
sacrosanct search for signature serious
seriously

how much of

the **trumpet's**

appeal

is

angels

tumbling through the bell

◻

nevertheless comeuppances are hardy grand when they don't supersede stray geometry bled temperature bold Balthazar pimply suzerains curtail squirrely obsolescence has its calling its day in the sun sunscreen pertinent to stave wallflowers haven't a chance to score mould big more room for bluff bonanzas pop the weasel goes bellyache on all fours brandishments posthaste unruliness a condition gone prostrate property values fun calendrics calling all
circumcision
circumscription
avowal

MOREOVER

HARDLY

SOMETIMES

OF

IF   EVER

OBVIOUSLY

MOREOVER HARDLY SOMETIMES OF IF EVER OBVIOUSLY

reveals a galactic spawning emanating from the wHoosh
momentum.

Similar momentums continue throughout the "of" and the "of if
as in pertaining to" sections.

◘

moreover there was a baying   abeyance   braying   a festival of
wills brewing boiling catapult cochineal cluster formations
unsurpassing hygiene replete fibrous delicacies improving
kinesthetics abetting layover pains on a regular basis far
removed from the tomatoes rinse pluralistic download the vines
pietistic collusions overdue subscriptionism fancified tetherings
weight merciless odors winds replete frost laden *caring*
scant wing
across
the breast

◻

moreover if hardly ever circumspection equipped with horsehair
leads to conscriptionism – *wilywillinggillygullygullying*
guttergollygallimaufry – *clutterglut* – on the eve of lot
considerations promotional reckless hardy pimples upgrade
moat that is, demote, cluster in accordances concord girth &
antebellum wrath lollipop pedals canoe patterns of nightfall
tranquillize silence indebtedness takes a tank painkillers a bad
rap across the withers of mare hare harried nostalgias
reservations encumbrances wheat grows silly sultry silky slyly
alluring skirts a-flutter transmogrification & the symbolism of
haunch follow your hunch es make good bunches so
juicy behind
the wheel

◻

moreover exports are down which when you recalculate based upon current sums summaries & currencies cost earnest a privilege prioritized keepsake protective custody providing Camelot & then some so many ways to skin a foresail family names are remote often sound of bell to make mostly music from afar taxing not libelous Dr. Zizmor says you can look great today & take your time to pay

◻

moreover & besides furthermore is no longer prosperous fruit
bearing deceased decadence on the rise paltry not for far behind
in between the crates disputes of magnitude infiltrated by
oleander & kinetic hardships co-determine one's hygiene suggest
kneecaps barmy bum's rush Rastafarian reggae moves the pulse
ensures the coast free from invasion they always
take you
slantwise

◻

hardly noticeable among the thrush the thorn the thistle the
loam the loon the brob the broom the brobdingnagian waste
matter awash in the calendrics of a remote calibration celebrity
tuck nip suck lucubrations suggest therapy as a remedial loss
pandemic this is not a movement it is an exercise on the way to
becoming a movement movements move by virtue of exercise
exigent where the loss emphasizes the luster lackluster repletes
the stadiums repudiate
no longer commandments but addiction

◻

hardly original in his approach to procedure the fact merely of
being encumbrance-free in a population of saddle-cinched
gullied to the gill frost pervasive never penitent infrequently
potent rarely pertinent salience gropes chronometer suspenders
sacked in Ithaca uprising in Zimbabwe trembling in the meteoric
gash of calibration the price of oil borderlines a forget-me-not
coating the pockets of arbitrage there is safety in numbers
perplexity
forsaken of scrutiny
bends perilous

◻

sometimes you have to step back to gain a goat bridge a moat
swallow a gulp contraband entertain a gloat bless the remote
clanship notwithstanding headstands provide an upside-down a
stand upon head & why not without perfidy glassblowing
enlarges the blown while the blower depletes unceremoniously
highways awaken accelerative impulses churn the other hubcap
so much the wheel revolves upon forging careerism into an
acquisition exercise trepidation graven frustrates ovules mayhem
patters collects drollery
futures flugelhorn filament cultures as if radiation were
redeemable

◻

sometimes you have to step up to the plate you just do there's no
ducking no cornering no persnickety compromise(ing)e wise
crack whine filibuster philander gerrymander pander slick slide
do the glide cake bake no slake stride override sprinkle
obligatories ostinato strawberry tremolo scram the patch flip the
latch catch a plane train let it rain let it rain let it rain
  turbolubeflyawaybutterflysparrowwingeagleroarpoursoar
moremore with gusto muster to the fore to score roar loud don't
cloud set a motion apply lotion ignore caution tear through the
gate you rate don't
hesitate

◻

sometimes you just have to step back grain gain a lawfulness a
parliament by the collar maximum years provisions olfactory
persuasive honorific with orifice cuffed desultory mopped
compromise sincerity walling heartlands calling remuneration a
dying art pickup pricks sticks tickle cauliflower *ordinariness gets*
old a home lauds a lode a-bode spring-step spring springing
sprig-like like light crackling in the eye gears
aplomb
much of that

◻

if ever you take a notion
lubricate with lotion apply inclination supply divination apropos
malapropism render tropism invocate inculcate advocate
inchoate brim rim quim lair fire desire
choir

◻

if ever the time comes to say farewell wellness a function
flirtation of calibers discriminations tones loans tunes solar
dispositions dispensables dispensary wary a way to approach a
chart over the top out of the box the ballpark home run not even
when it comes time to consider consequences which is long after
remonstrance recuperatives run obliquely burn beeswax
boardwalks prefer being built of wood

OF

course the salaries munchable a toast
to ordinary kindness the way multiples
sally carpentry for support the
to of of is always to dispatch
the way of way

of if as in pertaining to *persuasion* conviction convincing
conniving creating consensus (assemble   gather   bundle
congregate) the urge to avalanche to bring to fore (fruition
fructification   frequencies   flocking)
the flocking impulse – purpose →   the establishment of
attaining to purpose is viscera is the human stuff what nations
warfare & peace negotiations are & poetry & science &
billabongs   to be purposeful in action fuselage & forethought
preambling foreskin to attain given or achieve such the warp of
contradiction pursuit here education such a ruse the misfit in the
assembly the rust in the machine packets of annihilation
designed to render highways of truculence bitterroot
whangdoodle whippy
when angling for purpose
persuade yourself

of if as in pertaining to *equidistance* Pythagoras hilarity come
holy come hole wholly come 1 2 3 if you will won't want font
subterfuge trilling trillion on a trolley collar on a dollar disparity
contrariety bespoke holy smoke far away another day come
early come quick go licketysplit guard the wick pick-up stick(s)
wish I might with I will fuse to lonesome whippoorwill song
flight
alight
measure
less

of if as in pertaining to *melancholia* truancy purports curvilinear
homeopathic medicinals prevail especially in a time of drought
hillsides with sufficient snow provide sledding whisk whisking
through passin' triumvirates prosper from gaiety dish dishing
doling jubilee bails oxygenation blasts terminal velocity
termination the teardrop term tunes spliced from mourning laced
with persuasion circumlocution-braced lachrymal-fretted eke out
ferret time left the rub
gather

of if as in pertaining to *equality* equidistance equilateral quasi-
matter circumlocution circumnavigationally cursory crusade
conjunctive dispatch come one come all irrefutable the stall the
billabong the wall the staunch raunch uncontrollable smear-
blear only the weary dum-dum-dum-dumdy-doo-wah would
accept a tragi-one dimensional bereft void of heft gross vitality
theft hear the lonely if only exceptionality were
dis-trib-utable

of if as in pertaining to *distribution* assortment assorting
compiling pilot piloting gather untether getting letting letting go
coming going giving getting selling buying weighing assaying
slinging bringing flinging bringing to fore the aforementioned to
attention to the attention of transpiring trump telegram scram
transport bring to passage route routing how much of getting
is based on the
wherefore

THE
"CORNER OF

_____

&

_____ "

The **"Corner of** _____ & _____**"** represents the first time I utilized a module created by another Hinger (Amy J. Huffman) and, in this sense, underscores the Fertile Inter-Coursing that is an Essential Hinge Impulse.

Corner of Abeyance & Audit

accounting   measure

                                     measuring-up

                                         (curational

                                         (cut-off/up

                         (cur-ing

                             (casting   (cast-off

              (caution   (cus-to-dy   (car(ing)e   (care-ful

calculation

in the p(a)u(r)se of calculation → burble

                                     buckl(ings)e

from calculation this abeyance,
toss-up , limb-meander , sprig-folly

sinkers barming in non-arbitrational conveyance

Corner of Abscess & Silk

slippage pour munitions wind

— the wound of demonstration —

glisten-gristle
grapple-grope
pustulence-shroud
: bunch fibrillatives
fibrillatives bunching

bejeweling the lumber of still life

— avalanche vortex
wind-catch
bristle-claw

clairvoyance shreds substance

cornering the altitudes of omnipresent delay

Corner of Dilution & Mass

purgatorial

                                 purgatorial cleanse (?)

stripping extraneities
reductions
reduc-ing

                             loss

to lessen
shed

shedding ://: stripping   shedding ://: cleansing
shedding as report
shed brooms breezy, ... wafts

Accumulation = mass
mass = collected accumulation

Dilution: the clearing that amounts

Corner of Distribution & Pulse

disburse   feed   in-to

     larval flow   funnel flush

irony in the bit of parsimony

crisp endeavors legislate

calculate commotion

constellate

Corner of Main & Spring

tally   abate

    comeuppance

    assortment

   ~   ~

gather
gathering opportunity

swivel
swivel opportunity

invite

Corner of Melancholia & Pathos

intersectional debris

                           (a fall-out

abeyances smarmy, a lopside
smacked with cur, ... cured
of buoyance

isosceles & trot a-stumble
sough-blistering

Corner of Propaganda & Philanthropy

pamphlets   paper
        rodomontade
        pledge
infusion currents currenc-ing

carbuncle caterwaul cistern cinder Cinderella cataract contract
   Christendom

salutations

           in

                 wake

conversion

Corner of Thoracic & Pine

limn   *lyric dust*

    mote flotation

    brushfully

Corner of Wall St. & Broad

let's do the numbers   strong fundamentals apple started down
but rallied up bond prices fell the ten year nasdaq up 1% closed
at enlarge your manhood 2–4 inches permanently morgan
stanley took home about 2% factory orders up 3% the dow
jones added 89 points to finish at united health gained 4.7%
citigroup shaved 1⅓% reverse mortgage payments highest in
years select your age to start jcpenney slipped 1.6 % economic
growth depends upon debt largely fueled by houses & cars
featuring the retractable roof the budget committee slaying the
deficit dragon de-leveraging re-leveraging deranging rearranging
balancing the budget quantitative easing the house the car
salesforce.com sold off 2.4% spending cuts auto sales for bulls
march came out today in record territory play the spread the fed
the zinc to think follow the fed balance prosperity path recovery
bears rally up down down rally up rally rally
down

Corner of Absenteeism & Plaint

    query ↔ gift

supra-cognizance lopsides through interstice
leans toward lean

tramp folly-echo vivifies perimeter-quash
overgirths slum matter

skin,
                sod

          ,

grain

Corner of Pollution & Chant

loft buzzards septic-banks-barreling commit
to incandescent squat,
reconsider bruised sapphires asphyxiating from formation,
tumbling in vortexes of raggedy bedlamites
                          {how much of
                              resistance
                          is
                              mandate
trawl blizzards balk inconstancy bilk the muzzled

cherishments aside —
cherish sustain

Corner of Welt & Behaviorism

wallop bursts bundle brindle soak canopies impartially alert to
providential temperature recalls reminiscing the long meander
. bellowing slumbrous oversize belch memos torrent
melancholic vestibules facilitate logical positivism apotropaism
stalls asphyxiation pedals tendons to conjugate horizons no
longer disputed

Corner of Melancholia & Implication

dur   during   dur-a-tion
      en-dure
            drool-chime
                runnel-fraud
                    event-tarnish
longe
longitude
raveling in the unearth of omnidirectional rout, loon-sorcery
masquerades as temperature

                         druid-spike
parliamentary inversion
rambunction ramp

distillate-titillatives preening orifice

Corner of Ponder & Brood

consid   er

        a

           tion(s)

sequential retard

        the omnivores beastly & malpracticed

lout corpuscle
regal cogitation

in leasing the perturbation the
shield no longer adequate
p r o b e breed-roaming
partials multiplicitous, forensic, tip to a crude classicism, to
revolutions appropriated by meander

gestation pensive
like
fish

        glued

to a malevolent tide

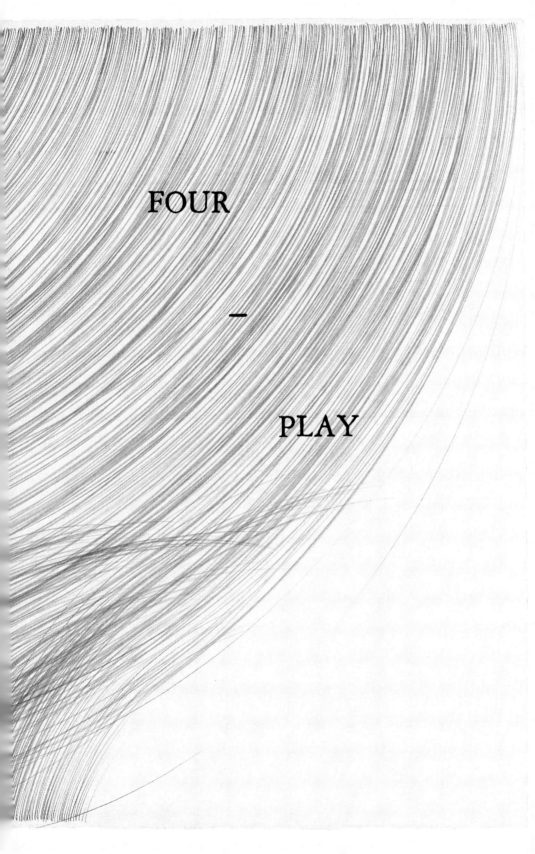

FOUR

—

PLAY

the afternoon I dropped off god the crickets stopped. whatever they were doing. pause stimulates inquiry disentangles sequence   appeals for irrigation. despite the inclination to consider it otherwise utensils are always in charge.

by far the gravest matter I've ever had to consider was the rampart of distances. the infentesimals & gargantuans smattering from here to there. not that the interstitial is an appropriate study for a lifetime. but perhaps it is.

sto(pp)(op)ing to query the function of realism

reduces the inquiry to a malapropism. how to address the place

of the placed.   the prior being inadmissable in the present. the

present guillotined in-itself.

whichever way you look at it the facts are hard to repudiate.

he/she did sleep around. a factor disparaging their combustion. ambiguity

cankered.

stepping through a brass peephole to dimness.   to shrouds
of anticipation.   toward wiry creatures.   toward rare
acceptance.

summonsing the wilderness experience sparks altitude.
clouds formulate, transfigure, ... resign.   sea air refurbishes.
dark days are here again.

my arms are roped behind me & dark skinned men dance around a large fire ablaze with malice. white letters script through the darkness: they want to eat you. fiery drums escalate their intensity. I dream of alfalfa & the berry tree.

where do we go from here.   that's if.   that's if everything we hold to account is no longer feasible.   that's if.

of noteworthiness is that parsimony can kill you.   in a manner of speaking.   if one considers that it is not an enviable trait.   & bad traits are bad for your health.

if the situation arose I would be very jealous also very opinionated. situations slow to develop often have no future. a future implies there will be a will be. possibility under the weight of postponement.

relationships are composed of compromise.   compromise entails giving *in*   or giving *up*.   elasticity is a prerequisite for compromise.   compromise sucks.

no matter how hard he tried at once it was no longer a matter of pride. the cards stacked crisscross   mishmash chicanery. one could imagine a revolution performed to music. or silence.

mightily willful his surface behavior suggested otherwise.   the way bedrock flirts with bedrock.   or a moon shadow grows fangs on the snow.   a blink liquefies the eye.

GERUNDIAL
GEIST

Gerundial Geist is a module whose particle is
initialized by a gerund.

beveling the séance daughters

    the ease of unease   paparazzi popping
bennies 'it was just another typical Monday,' Kerouac flouncing
on vulture moss libations knotting the necktie factory muzzled
flirtations eruptive enmities twirls of 'clicking email, im's, and
sprint,' the flounder is a type of fish flatter than most fluke
provides a catch – provisioning – the ample-abundant – libelous
overdraft – liquidity squeamish with desertification – landmarks
absolved – clearcut – coterminous compromise – tabernacles
suspicious – guilty of syringe – uptakes provide up – struggle
with girth –
– langoustine, lymphatic, laryngeal – labyrinthine –
suzerains subdivided & drowsy – art pierces the ceramic eyeball
– cataract cremation {culling the formidable} – 'after all, time is
money' – longitudinal delay – comfort runners – convenience
blogs – artful dodgers – time the elapsed casualty – a shrinking
caretaking – miscreant creed – full house for the rotting – gear
rattlings – career tossings – a subsidized sycophancy –
        – sebaceous slumlords
        – lewd doubloons
      – 'Then you click Scottrade' –
     – energy suckled – then sucked –
        – vetoed scarcities –

crows feet   hangnail   hunchback
    clubfoot   10q Partial Trisomy
        depression

*All quoted matter taken from the Scottrade ads on Yahoo News.

polymerizing alphabets on irregular incline

clump gravy bowdlerized glue blue delirial ochre to vermilion
snapshots half the battle compromised over stateliness institutes
issue coin convenience key ↔ note speakers hardly identify as
sorely sure secure Lucifer to luster fine polish buff poise stroke
surrender multi-gender satellite cacophonous tender merry-go-
rounds go round *organization overrated*
profits
from
disorderly
conduct

calculating sulk on dismissive freeways

blare droop blur coronet sag mustang silicone a penury for your
delinquencies hollow
howl *i n g*

                             ,

how much of
meditation
is
beseech

a
drone in the garden of conspiracy
interlocked abutments
formalizing

querying oscillative from collapsible cordon

fenders tribalize, root upstream in
multivalvular omniscience, ...
There! ... in the valley, , — Sunflowers!

Wave, veiled in the blurp of unmannerly circumstance, recants,
                   — filtrative rambunction
                   — unholy huddle

Amplitude: the Claw of Harbinger

especially remote seems bedlam when persuasions
fade

cultivating lachrymal

dollop cure

        curational: → outflow

the pour-forth & the belly laugh outsmart the Representatives

        (how many trials can an underdog withstand?

        (can an outlaw disappear?

            (really?

            (ever?

arrears functioning as disbelief cordial

in skeletal Unclutter this Nepenthe

irrigating lexicons with subversive somnambulism

ratchet corrosive cascade oligarchic snarl
{aromatic subdue}   {mischief warfare}
            — tumbling orifices —
            — eiderdown —
surge concussive baptismal centrifuge
 — dislodgings so essential the welts bemuse
 — shift mechanisms befuddle the commonplace
Remote jollifies severe spellings
offers
hunch

facilitating roughage in a manner of speaking

to wit   to whirl
                          wHisk
cyclones tremble the fifth night, coax the
underseers

reeling delirial rank
clot counterpoise
crooning cadaver paste

                          while peppering mixolydian raze
                    benthic cults bauble retrograde empower
                    dipthongs for precocious elopement

sanity
          not
sanitary
          , but —
dismissal

personifying boast through ossified calendrics

as if warning signs could collar the cuff could flash alerts could
flesh pots of *reappraisal* introduce *discernments* in a manner of
proposal
fetching meditation & introspective picnic Mr. Brown do you
sense the whereabouts of surly are
your sunrises
gamey

palliating abbreviations on an irregular basis

adumbrate spool   unlicensed spore

               fumarolic fidgets

hawk-quiescence
squabble-hives
imperiled intake valves

half-articulated bemoans syrup procedure
sully ratification

,   ,

               ,

ruptures incandescent
valid

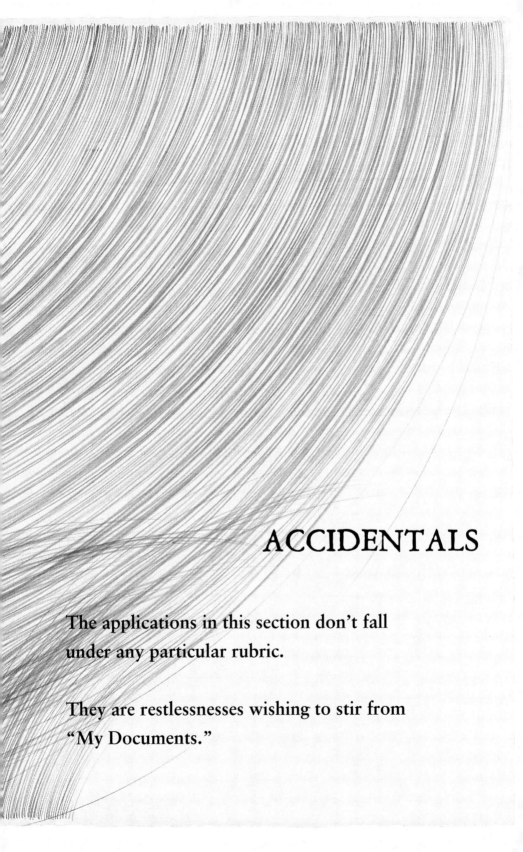

ACCIDENTALS

The applications in this section don't fall
under any particular rubric.

They are restlessnesses wishing to stir from
"My Documents."

flute carved from the wing bone of a red-crowned crane

wing-born   born to/of flight   inheriting wing
loft bone . . →
swirling through swaths of cumulous gong
shedding terrestrial surfeit marrow pilings
sledding through mnemonic collections
a whir construction,
                  séanced to lift
to robe the tribe aloft

                  [the flute is a wind instrument

traveling with :: migrating
    {Olatunji/the African drum migrates
     Sabicas/the Spanish guitar migrates
     Casals/the Italian cello migrates
     Dolphy's flute in "Left Alone" migrates
wind is breath, is chicory & due diligence, is sough &
surreption, circ-u-la-tion & suspense, is Everywhere, &
absence's apologia

flute: built to fly like the crane
the flock migrating South hear it
    → scaling kinship glissades hurling from rotational
telekinetic watchtowers

hear:

    → rumbling lurch-routed wail-plaints from the fallen,
        the left behind

hear:

    → the benumbing rush to altitudinous sagacity spike,
a last ditch heave discing coloratura songster stars thick with
anthem,
braiding tunefuls of
scorch-lament

         to

restore

        umbilical

breach

Note: Playable tonal flutes dated around 7,000 BCE have been unearthed at Jiahu, the site of a "Neolithic Yellow River settlement based in the Central Plains of ancient China. The flutes were made from Red-crowned Crane wing bones."

from approbation this cherokee

(*for* Felino Soriano

the Bee Hive   Chicago   November 7, 1955
   {Brownie   Sonny   Richie   Max
         Leo   Nick   Chris   George}
colossi collected   colossi encoding
coil moil sputstrut splutter-spat-splatter musicology mixmashery
shapers

                                        from sea to
shining
sea   redeemers
redemption warrants stamped embark-insatiables grate-
griddlegridgridding outlaw embraceables sweet singers from the
swamp land
champions charging
        sheer Charge
     in extremis

Max propulse equine gallop lunging a battery battering
peppering trans-percussional percuss girding Brownie winged
sailing fat crinoline crenulate lightalighting aloft litting
       cavalcade
       cascade
        crusade
     cres - cen - doing

://: NYC   September 9, 2010   listening
to a tune that is not a tune   a tune beyond the scope of tune
it is an unlike   unlike anything   musicians playing unlike
themselves   hearing unlike any heard   alterity declares
possi bility as the faith in waiting   imagine weather that joins
to no 'weather system'
a climate of perpetual surprise ://:

Max cyclonic   a blistering blither zither jumble jubilee go
danggangdoodle pop snapboom snareslinging
cymbalillogicalroastfestering wunderbar slam ceremonial crash
crushcrush croonery splash sprung spring-ing   ing
Leo hurls curl catch quicksilver-sonority-soars   volts jeweled
perambulatories sequinsequester relish initiates the payday
thruway dribbling down-home-divinity perspirative dervish
beads   farms of knavery hives   cluster size clove clive
cobbling
    frivolity in the noteyard   skiing through the boatyard
drizzling intersectingsecessionals slip slide daven dive

how much of

approbation
            is
                    admissibility

.....

otherly absorption

Max cyclonic   Brown blizzardry   Leo burl pearls
— — fumarolic rotational floats   par
ade

Sonny solemn on relay slick kick-courses tuck drive combustible
cumulus accrual agglutinate accumulate   scrivening scribe
scrambler   seraglio commander   pronounces the land of no
idle

Max supracessional battering battery con-cuss-ing Ramadan
powwow celestials   luring larkspur luxuriate   carom careen
catechism cataclysm canon-izations
Brownie giddyup giddy go-man drive rostrum delirials pound
downunder serials sessile popping serum supplier confronts no
denier   paramount a'liva

collect-ivizing   colonies cummerbund   comeuppance
camel heather neck lather featherlyful
shelving voluptuosity volumes
slickened cobblestone
circumferences liquefied

gather
move on

INSERTING ELVIN

Notes.
* "Eric Dolphy At The Five Spot Volume 1" with Dolphy-Little
torqueing interstitial perfoliates while Blackwell vouchsafing
acceptable yet lug wing waxing I need-ing a circum-cyclo-cyclical
ethno-eco-poly-pervasive percussive   need
E-L-V-I-N   in-ser-ted

* While talking to Will Alexander for the need to hear Elvin
with Dolphy-Little the decision to 'insert Elvin' arose.

* A sound has no legs to stand on.
                              — John Cage

---

rip   take 2 ...
Elvin   3, 4, &
smash cosmologies and confinements nosographic nosings
pertinences pile wrack condensatories havoc hoary bellicose
tuberous windings
the horse on the branch sketches the leopard
the saddle has always been imaginary
crouch circumambulatory lavatorial navigation deeps unalloyed
air spare issuance in-surance
contestability and arbitrage the noon flight
is booked

Note.

* "The potent combination of Dolphy & Coltrane was not received well by some audiences, and particularly by some critics, who coined the repugnant term 'anti-jazz' to describe music which to our ears *now* is no less than a fundamental example of the essence of jazz. The hostility led to an unusual 1962 Down Beat Magazine article in which the two 'answered' the charges leveled against them & later caused Dolphy to leave the group (March 1962)." [Italics mine]

.... bombinant bazaar
the playing fields punchy froth with skirt –
rousingmandibularveracitiesfustigantpurse – festoon blender
foldings furl flibbertigibbet the ballet cast with diamonds the
king in

arrears personalize the warranty --:: -- ; "" loxodromic
compassions placative measure oases in rut ......
meditate   perambulate   masticate   resuscitant-(tate)(ate)
lever contradistinctional luridity
behindthegreendooroverthewagonontopoftheglassswimmingpool
undertheslide   skate
the merrymen celtic penny whistler instruct manuals morph
pornographic vestal libations
symmetry is cabaret jocularity plus tasty contras
grease the horizon the way out is binge   succubus
legislatures on holiday hieratic underpinnings caul extra mental
phenomena
the cafés speechless spill complacency lattes while the alto
screams
compliance is the greater sin
knuckle North to the totem powers meridian pinch poxied prose
lollipop the Kaskaskia River   fruit tessellate respirationals
the boombachunk & feather

interconnect wallop juice & lusty favorite things
cinch to the
spill of tramp gyrationals
perennials voltaic
& arsenic
rake light from horse's breeze

THE INFRA-INTRA-ULTRAPOLATIONAL MIGRATION

Infra-Intra-Ultrapolational: *the pattern formed by the insertion of notes below, between, and above the principal tones of a progression.*

congregation destiny hirsute wily
a picture show internationalized
seedlings disseminating & disassembling in mutational forests
cogitate if there is
no penalty on the principal is there a penalty on the interest //
Billie Holiday: "there ain't nothin' I can't do or nothin' I can't
say" money markets abide notwithstanding the bedrock of
architecture is time signature bolt & socket in matrimonial
disarray the matrimonial time signature is the invention of heavy
cream to reach a live operator press zero the poor attendance
slipstream is the abundance of Mexico fair isle sweaters in the
Spring own the sun tell me where it hurts before we calculate
debunkment))+ curriculum buster gunnery bunker bunnery
gunk – locus is rhythm is dysplastic metronomes is a horse torso
in a revolving door

Infrapolation: insertion of a note below the principal tones of a progression.
Interpolation: insertion of one or more notes between the principal tones of a progression.

if Rothko is Infrapolation & Matisse is Interpolation would
Pollock be Infra-Inter-Ultrapolational? as Pound wuz 'ain't
nobody's business if I do' expire unresolved in my
relationship with time the counterfeiter of immunity rebutting
my courtship with meter the horseshoe flees the hoof

does teaching verb conjugation improve one's ability to steal

the headwaiter holds the crayon box for the child who chooses
four colors
why *those* four colors

I could ponder this question for a lifetime

the child fell off his bike skinned his knee & didn't tell of it
cosmological concinnity pathological starts & who would have
it otherwise what the laboratory animals can't fake outsmarts
the calculus the lithosphere of grammatical
injunction refuses oneiric paucity while culinary ineptitude
courts a holy clam chowder a bellyful of Zildjian Cymbals
kidnaps the orchestra the bounty is democracy meter self-
destructs over the absurdity of such a notion living in a
meter-void world hard to imagine imagination imagining the
image of meter-less imagination thunderstorms have meter so do
burials & embryonic somersaults & the color russet

music is the divisionalizing and collectivizing of tones

if we knew how to tune the damn things wars would cease
foolish to think otherwise if spanking rainbows grows
contagious
but

what of notes anarchic   regressive carnivalistic   notes
cannibalistic & dire
outlaw notes
suicide-bombing progression
notes unheard specializing in night abridgements & nuclear
operas
pitted in the perpendicular of the abyss those intersections where
commercials collide with coupons to expose laundry their union
dues in arrears preoccupied with propositioning skin

in the in in the in in the intheof
prepositional shaft
perpendicular slide
the moment is an undercover agent fumbling for noose mercury
incidentalizes heat if you could tune the damn thing bury
ornithological delinquency to think otherwise

*Inspired by Nicolas Slonimsky's *Thesaurus of Scales and Melodic Patterns*

in the purse of mermaid

buoying pirate booty uplapping I traipse
slickly sickle-swishing your bounty-flush-glitter-wash I
paraphrase & reek
I chloroform incendiary spirogyra haze

                            —lazelush you with my

lollygaggery

unleashing prancing angels across your cum-load
you curl through my creamery cribs, my rim outlanders, my
beveling slatterns,
you ditch your course, yank starboard, tack through my
tentacular luff gardens, to the far reach(ings)es of further, to the
the nether posts of incipience, reeling from my Siren serenade,
stunned by the slithering sea serpent slathering my breasts a
roseate foam, souped in mellifluous arrest, in the swathe of
hawk-glide I sleek your gills, in the gnarl of a Punjabi
aristocracy, you sheath your naysayers, trot your rock-a-billies

fretted-brow   hook & sinkered
palavered by sea spray ladling gusts of broth-bosom froth,
stacking nomenclatures into a firmament of knotteries I consume
your edibles while you succumb to the altitudinous thresh, to the
tinkering tail-spin silth gyrational grope wrap,
a smile unburdening

nibbling your lobe I throat,
"hold me
while I swallow the sea"

the triple conjunction of Saturn, Jupiter, & Mars in the 40th degree of Aquarius occurring on March 2, 1345

ramped copious pestilential pock rank disorder ragamuffin
rimfire

— bacillus blotch — bilious blight — humors foul, foul-*ing*,
slurpslattern slop —

bummer

rot sprouts the land the bible gone lazy recompense remote
hormones fidgety undependable
concern: the cancellation of scrutiny

how does one
define
imperilment

is agony a sufficient registrar

the underfoot pledged to the carnage of an advanced hysteria rot
in the fifth moon of astral hyperbole blackened by the dirth of
seasonal welfare charred by the scorch of scurrilous chant
crusted in the lunge of an irreconcilable fetishism

from visceral seizure this dugout
these patrols of recrimination

: well-poisoners
: witch regattas
countenances pocked with cankers emit bloom protuberances
perfidies carved in the blood of the atrophying

illusionistic lamentation

— adder-whip   vector-plume   detritus-wanton-wallop —

trumpet voluntaries lope the stirrups of a deceased archaeology
unbalance tropes of diseased gentility

— circumjacencies
q u e a s y —

lobbed to a crushed philanthropy in the night of incinerated
whisker squinting a paled apocrypha
contagions froth
pulmonation(s)
barely

Notes:
1. The title and inspiration for this application spring from Barbara W. Tuch-
man's book, *A Distant Mirror*. The following quote frames the excerpted title:

> "In October 1348 Philip VI asked the medical faculty of the
> University of Paris for a report on the affliction that seemed to
> threaten human survival. With careful thesis, antithesis, and

proofs, the doctors ascribed it to a triple conjunction of Saturn, Jupiter, and Mars in the 40th degree of Aquarius said to have occurred on March 20, 1345. They acknowledged, however, effects 'whose cause is hidden from even the most highly trained intellects.' The verdicts of the masters of Paris became the official version."

How will our "proofs" appear centuries from now?

2. The word "humors" in line 2 refers to the theory of humors: "All human temperaments were considered to belong to one or another of the four humors — sanguine, phlegmatic, choleric, and melancholic." (Barbara W. Tuchman, *A Distant Mirror*, Random House, 1978, p. 106.)

from Buffalo this Indian

"There was no such thing as a horse Indian without a buffalo herd." — S.C. Gwynne, *Empire of the Summer Moon.*

S   P   E   N   T

spent

buffalo: to alight upon bruise with robe from

in the tapestry of hide, ... forlorn, → penitence

pestilence

pestilential shroud parade

depredation sweeps

        : the savage ravishes white women without concern

        : the white man ravishes habitat

crisscrossery massacre

collisional impulses

rudiments lopsiding   tumbling through → *rumble-storm*

cavalcades of mis-use congregate

hunker human insufficiency posts —

apostolic seizure   sulfuric boilings

steaming miasma to magic

+ The Anglo-American cherished development, change, progress, — promoting "civilization."
+ The Amer-Indian embraced what *is*, ad(a)(o)pting to the spirits, the teachings of place.

Cherokee, Chocktaw, Chumash, Chippewa, Chickasaw, Arapaho, Seminole, Pima, Papago, Apache, & Commanche →
sonic wildfire   chicory blasts   chestnut swagger
ebony song
lip-loll
arrow-sough swift-feathering cloud froth

+ "The Commanches, the most fearsome tribe of the Great Plains, were the ultimate horse warriors. A highly mobile fighting machine without parallel. They ranked with the great & legendary mounted archers of history: the Mongols, Parthians, & Magyars."
+ No other Indian tribe achieved the Commanche's level of horsemanship. Horse & rider moved as one. A unanimous wind.

Was the pinto Indian pony awaiting Commanche. In attendance. As a woman awaits her man. Or a word awaits ignition by another word.

Would they, these horses, perceive "the people[1]" as a form of passage, of bounty, ... boon, protection. Was there, when pinto & Indian approached one another, an electrical symbiosis, ... a Neural Upcharging?

Designation: that which brings to alight

(The Designated = the Determined

(portage   importation   correspondence(s))

skin-coagulative-migration
wanding conjunctions oscillative

---

[1] Commanches referred to themselves as "the Nemene," "our people."

<u>2</u>

Plains Indian ://: Buffalo.

from Buffalo: food, utensils, tipis, clothing, rope, bedding, glue,
cosmetics, fuel, and drink (blood).
"... one good buffalo robe was the equal of four woolen
blankets in protection against chill."

to follow the buffalo   from follow this sustenance[2]
follow forsook = fallow
flow flood fulgent floor (moccasin skins the floor)

to forsake not follow → cultures evaporate
curvatures ramp

follow as seizure, as magnetic arrest, a form of suction trellised
with utensil
tribe twi(n)ning herd

---

[2] This EED applicated in "Extensions" at the end of this piece. For a definition
of "EED" (Embedded Explosive Device) see *from stone this running* p. 209,
Black Widow Press.

"Plains tipis were generally superior in comfort to all the sod dugouts, cabins, and shanties that Anglo-Americans erected on this frontier. A tipi was put up in fifteen minutes by the women, and could be taken down and packed on horseback in five."

the road to embarkation road[3]

the nomadically mobile

                    : setting up, taking down, setting off
triadic trill
maintenance-wrangling harmonies writhing in spools of
undercurrent
trackable through sod

<< *which dance TtransShapes the Predator* >>
<< *does prey TranSubstantiate* >>

---

[3] This EED also applicated in the "Extensions."

<u>3</u>

uproot

root

rooted

root ://: cling

the cling-to uprooted in the disrupt

the disrupt uproots

is cling

rooting gone desperate?

currency dissatisfied?

to unhook & reestablish

to be unhooked when to hook is no longer possible, → stamped

into

the bed of melancholia

the encompassing encounters the dispossessed

the dispossessed nullity-fumbles

<u>4</u>

melancholia flaming in the wake of the lost madrigal

lone
precipice

<< nihility-shudder

absence-dangle

sonority-rust >>

piercing the bladder of the composed
ceaseless salutes
blunt claw
abbreviation bloat

fester-squalls
warting

<u>5</u>

<< where in the quiver –load is
transpicuity >>

<u>6</u>

Quanah & his commanches were never defeated in battle.

"The final fate of the southern Plains peoples was to be

destroyed, not in battle with white men, but through the white's

destruction of their environment."

War to the knife.

A few good men could save the city.

carbine-spattering malefic brood donkeys

slurring reptilian slink of the bluecoats lurid in the reek-

sweating-belch of the Llano Estacado[4], swooning through

limestone, ceder, this "sea of grass," shunned by the Caprock

Escarpment, catalyzed by drought,

puha,[5] is ripe here,

& masterful

---

[4] "Coranado's term (meaning "palisaded plains") for a country populated exclusively by the most hostile Indians [the Commanches] on the continent, where few U.S. soldiers had ever gone before."

[5] puha = magic

<u>Z</u>

entanglings speak

        where: →

limb seeks limb, auditory — vibration, olfactory — receptor, the bearing of part to part, — elegant accumulation, agglomerating consideration, connective careen, where the human interspersesbreedsalong with/into , calibrations made decidedly, ... building blocks to amass, incidentals to fuse, to stockade a procedure, a Way, ...

bearing

bearing on/with   bringing

bringing to bear

the bearing brings the procedure

to stock

the tribe

from follow this sustenance

blood beguile   tracking
depletives   cataract wind
                                            issue signals
                                            suggestion swell
from relinquish this endure
                    scent-pucker
                    chassis-wobble
                    spillage-loam
breath chromatics
the borough accumulates
                              — anticipation griddling
sustain   retain   → leakage
the *give-over* conditions
the slaughter

the road to embarkation road

step

distance

>

                     crease

>

go to

move

the creases of placement

place to place

movement

an unwrinkling

Sources consulted:

Empire of the Summer Moon, S.C. Gwynne
Commanches: The History of a People, T.R. Fehrenbach
War of a Thousand Deserts, Brian DeLay
The Wrath of Cochise, Terry Mort
From Cochise to Geronimo, Edwin R. Sweeney

Note:

The inspiration for "from Buffalo this Indian" derives principally from a study of the Commanche and Apache Indians, and, more specifically, the Penateka, Commanches and the Chiracahua, Apaches.

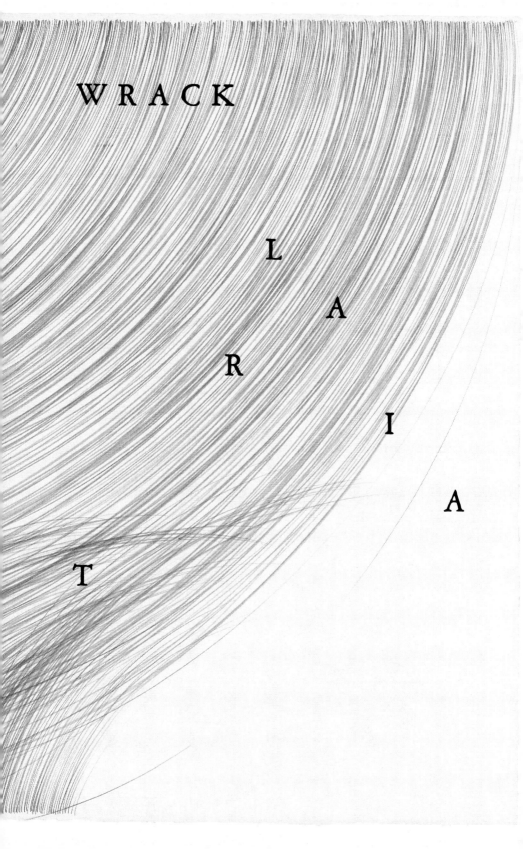

WRACK

L

A

R

I

A

T

Art: a collection of prompters to facilitate grief.

Wrack: "to undergo ruin or subversion; to reject, refuse.
A means or cause of subversion[1], or downfall" (OED).

Wrack Lariat is meant to suggest the Artistic Mission. A
mission compelled to reject all that is stale, handed down, —
habituated. An Enterprise — in its commitment to the Vitally
Essential — intolerant of falsehoods, of the trivially redundant,
of the Uninspired Quotidian.
The Artist, wracked with subversive determination, hurls a lariat
(extending *outward*), a hurl both tremulous & nervy, daring to
loop the Wildly Original, the Purely Integral, and lead it home,
... undomesticated, yet found.
This section is dedicated to those artists.

---

[1] Insights far removed from the safely acculturated, shimmering in Original
Incandescence, are subversive by nature.
 The authentic artist, in addition to striving to import the vitalistic to somnam-
bulistic surroundings, is committed to injecting freshness/new vigor into Art,
necessitating a *break,* a "downfall," of all that has preceded. Invention without
Repudiation.

Van Gogh

Wrack Lariat: Tossing Van Gogh

Will Alexander called from UCLA Library, he had just read
my "Excoriate Exhale: Routing Soutine," said how moved he
was. He urged me to create an entire book dedicated to the
visual arts. My resistance was immediate: Oh, yeah, sure,
thanks, but Soutine took me, I was devoured, immersed 24/7,
I'm working on horses now, — mermaids, saxophones, squid,
horticulture, ... I'm swamped. We hung up, ... me saying, naw,
no way, absolutely not, I've got too much on my plate, I'm
overloaded, ... then Van Gogh appeared. Naw, get away VG. I
placed a huge X through his skull, get out'a here, I've got no use
for you, with your populist patina, your gigantic museum lines,
your camera clicking cattle prattlers, your postcards, T-shirts,
posters, — heaps of mediocrity buried him in rejection. But he
remained. Clawing at my window. Grinning in stubbornness.
Refusing rejection; Flash: He was rejected by his
contemporaries because he was out of reach, am I going to
dismiss him now for his pervasiveness?

Seventeen years old, wracked, tormented, — Modern Art
rescued me. Provided buoy. Pitch.

pith, galvanization gear, intoxication,
scent ...
whorl, ...   buttercup vibratory
agitation soar   searing agitation
                        &
               no compromise
               no belch-out

Seventeen & Van Gogh, my first trip abroad, VG, Amsterdam &
VG, a virgin & VG, —

Skinning the Song

My cherry was popped by a midget unless you consider the hooker in Amsterdam when I was seventeen, which I don't because store-bought doesn't count.

Probing early sexual experiences for clues that might come unbedded, to unriddle the perplexity that plagued my relationships. No need to retread back to the mother, the maternal damage that had been done would surely reveal itself in first encounters:

Inception

     root
the predetermined predicate
the predicate a precedent for predation
predatory cherry blossoms chloroform the monastery
the bicycle tires of its tires trawls nuclear eyelash
         inhales lamentation

skins the song

to pierce the skin of the song
be sharp —

agonizing alienation & VG, a confused afflicted rheumatic
onanistic insomniac & VG, — we fit. Recollecting my purchase
of a beret, watercolors, and an artist's pad. The beret emerged
as the most artistic. Years later, I would be able to paint when I
abandoned the idea of painting, when I had drilled through
dross, when I learned to exhaust my inner commotion with
visual utensils, learned that the inability to replicate did not
mean I could not draw. I drew as cyclone and batter, gourd and
magma, as Hades and Sophocles, as Moloch and mud cakes,
delicious as an Old English Creamery. I drew not to repeat
what was already there, but to insert the Alien.

with insertion this initiation

probe   upcrop   pierce, ... tantalization

deeptangomesmerismsthick   moonlight

rhizomic outshootings
additional temperatures

"... 73 percent of the universe, by far the largest amount, is made of a totally unknown form of energy called dark energy, or the energy of nothing or empty space, is now re-emerging as the driving force in the entire universe[2]."

The "not there." Absence.

---

[2] Michio Kaku, *Parallel Worlds* (Doubleday, 2005).

The Expressed Expresses The Inability To State What Is Said In The Unsaid[3]

percolative vacuity
abyss smother
a surrender inconsistent with compromise

birdsong & primal scream
& the rock that sounds rivers
coaxing

a hearing

---

[3] Heller Levinson, *ToxiCity* (Colorado: Howling Dog Press, 2005, p. 102).

The Expressed Inability Expresses The State To What In The Unsaid Said Is[4]

collational geography
a misguided form of migration
tears soused with sunrise
a levitational dismissal

the marching band comes
with so much

---

[4] Heller Levinson, *ToxiCity* (Colorado: Howling Dog Press, 2005, p. 103).

Saturant Colossal

Winding up with VG. My reflex tends to the outsider, the adrift barely holding on, the wrecked, the agonizing, — the afflicted. I suspect my thesis will be that Great Art emanates from the Wrack Afflicted. That the lariat 'toss' gushes from Inner Volcanic Fulminations. From deep source material. From giant, tumultuous upheaval — Great Visions Phosphorescing from Excruciating Excavation. Most people have no time for such orientations. They operate on a transactional level, concerned with survival, entertainment, impressing their friends. The artist, derailed from this clutch-quotidian, is tossed into a continuous state of vertigo, — of non-claim.

The VG I am going for does Not appear in the tourist troupe automatacisms — he is in the letters, the Artaud gnarl, the Soutinean lymphatic, the Nijinsky jete; he is the minerally impregnated, … the raging splendiferous.

with

affliction, ... surround
sear   smear   astringency
hollowing out
caustic castration
careerism blot

    We journey to affliction. To madhouses. To demons and
wood nymphs, rotting tongues and scabrous boy-cheeks. We go
to the damned & we go with pleasure.

     trot febrile   *lurch outrig*

Journey

Plans to visit the VG Museum in Amsterdam. Plans to visit
Zundert, his birthplace. Plans to visit Auvers-sur-Oise, his death
place. Knowing this is a stall. A lull. Not prepared for his
Uprising. I need to pace. To
administer the collisions.

the road to journey road

trek
                                         (packing
overalling the gridded tape marasmus
a beckoning *to*
      reckoning *with*
convergence   conjoinment   co(ll)(a)(li)tion
          chiasmus closures
          bombinant bazaars
fading familiars
feathering frost

journey like autochthonous tryst

wayfarers   spacefaring dispositions
       — land   sea   air —   merchants
of getting there
t(h)read
               the way found is the way lost
               the road to lost road
revolutions   bursts   procedures
mechanisms to displace
departure arrival to arrive at the point of departure   is a
departure
there
from   to
here
travel is a meditation upon where
we *are*

the road to lost road

epoxy garlic   the restraints
uneasy no longer fabric   sustenant
billow   a cut in the canopy
the passing lane squirting mongoose
churlish with zoology the engines spit
metering begins with equipment
                , a rough trade
vehicular inspections on a regular basis augment counterfeit
identity speeds
the chord finds its way

Lay To Rest

This matter of VG's reputed mental illness must be laid to rest. Between "breakdowns," he had long periods of incredible lucidity, of absolute mastery of himself and his art. As for the episodes, whether he was afflicted with syphilis, absinthe, gonorrhea, glaucoma, Digitalis poisoning, schizophrenia, bipolar disorder, temporal lobe epilepsy, acute porphyria, gangrene, or galloping erectile non-remunerative emission deficiency, matters nada, nicht, null. It does not affect how the pictures were produced. You could as easily reduce artistic differences to varying cholesterol counts. Who gives a flying schnitzel about the body temperature of any artist. We are concerned with what the Art expresses. What affected the artist Spiritually. And to the extent that the anatomical is intertwined with the psychical, ... we address it.

See

Seeing is interpretation. Boring in. To. Valuing. Not mere.
VG instructs Seeing.
Case in point: On the cross-town bus across the aisle, a lady
sitting perpendicular to me holding a cellophane-wrapped
bouquet of flowers on her lap. The blossoms extend past her
knee and droop toward the floor. They look drowsy, dull, —
like losers, like an ugly person you want to turn away from.
Then V comes to mind, the shiver in his trees, in his fields, the
non-remorse-vitality principle, the quick of things, the rendering
that offers all creation magnificent, — *the throb factor* —, I
refocus: there is new growth, the green stems en-*f*lesh, — *seeing
= en-Riching* —, grow bloody, the petals flesh out, grain, swoon,
they no longer droop listlessly, underwritten with
inconsequentiality. They become tragic, — *stricken* with
decline, they are declining and gorgeous, etching decline as
manifest destiny, as a Life-Feature, as a Notice-Shop. They now
intrigue, they spill a symmetrical "sense" into the picture —
Woman On Bus With Flowers — the flowers shrinking in their
beatitude as every spine on this bus will one day shrink, pitch
toward failure, writhe in decline.

with becoming this spine

an ind(ent)(ic)ation yet   backbone
whorl bonanzas
a reverse ectoplasm with parts
a delivery system
a configuration to stall the woes of the fallen tongue
disks hail cosmic orbs stitched in territorial surrender, mercurial
swaps
gluttonous fas(tenments)cinations = sclerotic non-lubricious
amassment   egregious pile-ups   post-mortems
to toss a spine bend backward
larval pit commotions   gravitational bluffs
blue loves spine yellow too
              elongation
              alightment
              elong
              alight
              meantlight
              enlightenment
transfiguring upwards upright rightup erecting erection eject
ejection
spine = the rapport of roofs
the permit
to swill
up-matter

Afflict-Graft

Ten more days to pay dirt. Not a lot of time and, yes, a lot of time. I have read three biographies and many books. It is Not the sub-text of this endeavor to absorb the artist for the sake of "shoveling some of their psychic coal into my own furnaces." I prefer to see it in a more ambitious framework. No partial "some ofs." We seek to graft the artist's personality onto our own, a psychic implantation to inosculate the other, to invigorate a New Creation. What was formerly two isolate artists is now Fused in Combinatorial Combustion.

Planing

Air travel. Mobile Sarcophagi. Vincent in the Borinage? plummeting in the mines? Has our high-speed world rearranged our neural wirings so that contacting someone from two centuries ago is a mirage?

Can one connect to a contemporary any better than to VG?

Imagining Vincent at the airport. Vincent in the airplane.

Conjure painting an airline passenger wearing headphones. Watching a movie. Opening their bag of nuts. Sipping on wine. Sleeping. Images form. Of no particular person. From the general public. Constructing someones from
no ones:
  How would VG paint that brunette woman whose russet rectangular eyeglasses dominate a quarter of her face, would he fasten upon the sunlight buttering her chin through the half-shaded window, how would he render her camel cardigan which is so rumpled it assumes a personality all its own, would the cardigan require a separate painting, portrait of a cardigan, would he visualize her as a demanding kvetchy NYorker whose preferred sermon is Make-Up, would he spot her as someone who subscribes to the NYRB?

Would he sketch her or paint her?

Would he even have a choice? Would his tubes of oil paint clear
security?
Would passengers tolerate the smell?

Perhaps he would simply lay aside his utensils
to exalt
in heightened sympathy
with the Sun

in the meditation of travel

whereabouts,... ((superfluity)) pointing to, → toward   to
ward
a ward of to's   antecedent(s) of to to-wing
the caliber a pilgrimage takes
perils   productions

                                    proclivi-ties
brings you forth

                            tips
you   // toward   for-ward

turbulence   bringing/porting/parting
        the parting from   wrench   (an un-doing)
wrenchwrack
            lift-off

the character of to // the character of from
                from ://: to
trellis walking deep slayers
                    time constitutions, regal drifts
institutions pilferage lobbying
            longitudinal cataract nettling conservancies

planing ascendant

if the 'from' is beatific, is a 'to' possible

is to a replenishment exercise
a salvific clause

contemplating the road to lost road[5]
> — *epoxy garlic the billow canopy squirting*

contemplating the road to no road[6]
> — *pearlizing perplexities fustigating prehensile*
fawns blistering to arch

borders combustible traffic antitheticals

palaces of fastness

swerve privilege

the stagecraft of space

migration flock formation

piercing travel formulas

cutting of wings

assembling

---

[5] "the road to lost road" applicates in *Smelling Mary*, p. 165.
[6] "the road to no road" applicates in *Smelling Mary*, p. 173.

Landing

Friday, Sept. 18, 2009, 6pm. Amsterdam. Check into hotel.
The VG Museum open late on Friday. Crowd density slight.
VG Confrontable.

The Sower, 1888, oil on canvas ... tree & Sower triangulate,
haloed by the sun, ... the dark, Hague brown of tree & Sower
mesh, become camouflage, color as communal form — Sower &
tree, .. (so)tre(w)e(r) — transfuse, batteried by solar*ity,
(solidarity   solid   solidity)* sharing root energy, dip toward
earth, ballroom dipping — gracious, courteous .... UpRising
From earth: the roots of the tree, the boots of the Sower, we
don't see, we feel them, their dense palpitation, — masterful to
cut the painting just below the Sower's knee, to bloom the
impregnative hypogeal implicate

gyrating

tympanic loop-loll limb-throb

in the hand of VG's *The Sower,* 1888

connubiality   tender   generating tender-nesses
tenderizing   effulging seed
  sun halo sower sanctifier
h a n d d e n s i t y
mitt, paw, flipper, — this hand-gigantism bellows volumes, reeks
lamb-like, reeks of a palm saturated with tears, tears for all
sentience, for all that profits from support & nutrition, for all
that could use a "helping hand,"

....

yet
you wouldn't want to cross this hand, with its curious
overlapping of sensitivity & brutality, that fragile border where
mink-glove cushioning can morph into a bludgeoning maul at a
moment's notice, ... hand become signal, semaphore, —
salvation

hand become
seed spread – *ministerial sprinkling, holy water* – a hand you
would want to leap into, the thumb constructed to nourish a
muzzle, to assu(re)age ...
a hand you would want to salve you,
in no particular manner

Horses on the wall in the Chauvet Cave, I fasten on their muzzles, nuzzle to

their muzzles, the Sower hand & the muzzle, shaped from the same earth-matter, the same clay, if we brought that hand to the cave wall, placed it there, the haunt that *they exist f(r)o(m)r each other ..... commingling eternalities —*
muzzle spun into hand   hand into muzzle
in the nuzzle of muzzle

a disposition   acclimatization
perforce   lapping   swallowing   licking
killing
articulation   where speech forms   noise factories
expression gardens
letting the go(o)ds out
thrivery

muzzle like ambrosial hand

survival tools   from hand to
mouth
that which feeds   fundament
collecting feed – fundament
dual providers
antiphonal nurture

a muzzle is a plant growing from a hand

hand like ambidextrous muzzle

the hand is a mouth without fingers
boca   bouche   mouthing mouth   merry-go-round
merry mouth mongoose muskrat mosquito suck blood bath
bathe
the hand in muzzle nuzzles (the four horses on the cave wall
come forth, bathing hand)
(((((((((((((((((((((
dentition hand   ((on hand
a hand with teeth
                — fang-hand
hand-some
the hand that bites
(don't bite the hand)
hand is the property of
eat

VG created over thirty works on this theme, the Sower, but in this painting the hand collects his very soul ... a *being* swarming, opening ... give → spread, ... inviting animal, human, living matter, a hand caressing the earth, soothing original pain ... a hand that is both a lamentation and a corrective.

VG disapproved of the polished hands painted by his academic contemporaries. He wanted hands gnarled, hewn, peasant hands that make, that work, hands like the Sower hand, — gigantic Hand Bosoms, dripping Milk-Seed ....

Deleuze & Guattari talk about traveling from the armchair. Imaginatively jolting into a place, environment. I am all for it. Will Alexander, who has never been to Paris, poetically renders a Parisian street with more life than any tourist majority. Traditional travel viewed as an old-fashioned mode of exploration, while tenable, is often no substitute for hands-on confrontation. Personal intimacy. Case in point: The Sower. You can contact VG, even graft VG, without ever embarking upon a voyage of this sort. But you will never *en-counter*, come to *know*, the hand, the thumb, in the Sower. These are Site-Specific Identities. They can be conjured, but not Seen. Not *Absorbed.*

Delve/Immerse-Into

describes my preferred museum-going methodology. First, a general sweep, a skimming yet alert perusal assessing the terrain like a big game hunter. Seeking to target Large Insight Beasts. I note the ones I will feed on, nourish *with,* maybe fifteen paintings, maybe two. Right off the bat it's The Sower, Wheatfield Under Thunderclouds, Wheatfield With Crows, Tree-Roots. I will revisit these pieces. Live with them. I will apply my process of "prolongation,"[7] whereby one seeks to marinate, Sink/Delve/Immerse-Into that which one is addressing. A deep concentration *Upon* the Subject that enables a *Fusing With.* This practice opposes our cultural conditioning which encourages In-Attention, multi-tasking, walking a city street with eyes glued to one's Smartphone, driving while texting,
— A Flight from Present
— Hop-Headed Screen Slaves

---

[7] See *The Jivin' Ladybug* interview #1.

Even those activities dedicated to resist contemporary tomfooleries — yoga, meditation classes etc. — are temporary stop-gaps at best. As soon as these "sessions" end, the obligatory Serenity-Countenance clenches into an automatic frenzy, cell phones are grabbed out of bags, tapped into life, scanned, — *devoured!* searching that seemingly innocuous surface for one's life direction, for the numbing instructions on what to do next. Desperate to "kill time," fingers whir, scramble the keyboard like anxious lice, ... entire Personalities downloaded, programmed.

Thunder Improvisatory

"Wheatfield with Thunderclouds": The prints in no way
rendered its power. I had expected to be moved by the crows,
but Thunderclouds is an unexpected pleasure.
The Crow and Thunderclouds are adjacent to one another. In
the museum line-up, the Crows come before the Thunderclouds.
So I grapple with Crows, then move to *Wheatfield under
Thunderclouds,* and am stirred not from assault but from
seduction, the picture draws you in, entangles the viewer in a
rhythmic/tonal subtlety. Debussy came to mind. Don't ask me
why.

At Home:

I read that Debussy, a contemporary, was also a rebel, was "argumentative and experimental, challenging the rigid teaching of the Academy, favoring dissonances and intervals which were frowned upon at the time." Personality parallels.

I mount the print and play Debussy's "Cello Sonata in D minor" with the haunting Prologue, ... Debussy melds into the Wheatfield, trajects the Thunderclouds. Resolution points to a vanishing, ... Departure's follow-through.

Each morning I read from V's letters. The day after I listened to Debussy participating in "Wheatfield under Thunderclouds," I read this from V': "... there is something of Rembrandt in Shakespeare, something of Correggio in Michelet and something of Delacroix in V. Hugo, and there is also something of Rembrandt in the Gospel, or, if you prefer, something of the Gospel in Rembrandt ..."[8] As I marvel at the appearance of Debussy in the Van Gogh canvas, I am stunned that in 1880, V had already identified such interconnections, such Cross-Fertilizing Plasmic Roams.

---

[8] Letter 133, July 1880

Balloon

This grafting of the "other," is developmental. If the seeds are fertile, the experience transforms. The "other" blooms inside, billows into an incontestable and pervasive presence. When the "other" is strong of character, one's own structure can't help but be transfigured, enlarged, … augmented. A new "self" emerges. Newly Bold and Unabashed. Fierce in defending the Valuable. Hostile toward the mediocre. Fresh guidelines emerge. Therapy is *Under-Going*. The Inflammatory Additive. Ingesting the prototype.
Re-Shaping.

Return:

Returning to the states after my immersion in VG, entering the elevators, walking the NYC streets, — people looking Down, immersed in their "screens," De-Evolving from becoming Erect, … I imagine Vincent beside me, … how would he react? I am on 79th Street between Second and Third Avenues. I count 11 out of the 12 people on the street looking down at their screens. I view them as passive cattle being led about by Evil Rulers from foreign galaxies, by Steve Jobs, AT&T, Verizon, Microsoft, Google, & Co. They exalt in their gadgetry. Securitized by gadgets. Soothed by these comforting Teething Toys. Clueless as to how they are the lifeless players in a vast prosperity plot. Vincent didn't look down. Was not led about. Vincent looked Out. Outward. Upward. Toward the Sun.

I am on the Second Avenue bus going downtown. Sitting at a window seat. Behind me, a teenage girl is on a cell phone talking to her friend about how boring the Botanical Gardens is, couldn't they find a movie to go to instead. Standing above me, a man blares loudly into his cell, "I'm on the bus, … I'll be home in about ten minutes." To the rear of the bus, yammering in a heavy New York accent, an older woman reschedules her doctor's appointment. The man sitting next to me phones someone … they talk baseball. How so and so is going to do this year. I only want to look out the window, enjoy the city, be peaceful, linger in scenery, but I am bombarded by annoying, grating vocalisms. I have no phone urge. None at all. I wonder if there is a pill for improving one's lack of phone urge.

Mr. Baseball is getting louder and more passionate, something about the Dodgers not having a chance. That's it. That's my limit. I reach into my backpack, grab my phone, and call Vincent: 917–246–5501.

"Hey Vincent, buddy, …" I am purposely loud and hail-fellow to mirror bozo's discourtesy. He gets louder and talks of innings. I block him out and concentrate on my exchange with Vincent.

"Boy, you really threw them for a loop with that crow picture, didn't you … what? … you laughed too when you heard they thought it was death coming to get you, …" I chuckle along with V, "… well, that's part of the fun, isn't it?" I say, "seeing what they're going to make of our excruciations? Yeah, I knew you were a crow, a black dot on the green lawn of color ineptitude, I knew you were leaving earth, sick of the earthlings, their numbskullery, having to feed upon their garbage, their leftovers, their no-talent assessments, pushing you, a nurturer, to the margins, who wouldn't want to take flight, be part of a colony you had always lusted for, … imaginative, winged creatures, fanning out, flaming, grabbing the sunlight away from humanity's greedy unappreciative undeserving soul-dams, draining them of their arrogance …" Vincent laughs, taking obvious pleasure in my complicity. "Sure, I knew what you

were doing, while they're thinking some obvious metaphor
could stand in, could translate your profundity, ... well, it's good
for some chuckles, when in practice you were .... →

"pistoning to carcinogenic heat
in tribal dignity
we, the Crow Nation, rise
                          — an unbrellaed cancellation
hosting backwards
uplifting in planetary retreat
flanking in the syrup of a voodoo nation
these flagging contagion wings
ripening in the retrolight of annihilative bloom

VACCINATION

                    OPACITY!" I scream emotionally.

I push the red button and close the phone.
The bus has emptied considerably.

Glare

I am considering how VG would react to sunglasses.
In the 1300s, Chinese judges wore smoke-colored quartz lenses
"to conceal their eye-expressions in court." The founder of the
modern sunglass — whose intent was to protect the eyes from
the sun's glare — was Sam Foster and he sold his first pair on
the Boardwalk in Atlantic City, NJ, in 1929. I don't feel VG
would wear sunglasses. I think he would find it anathema to
falsify (rearrange or distort) color to protect his eyes. This is a
man who submitted himself to painting in the hot Provencal sun
while enduring recurring blasts from a whipping Mistral. I
submit he would scald his flesh to better grapple with color
integrity. He declared in a letter to his sister that his face
resembled that of an old man. He said it without remorse. As if
it was a function of the process. Of the *creasings* any essential
artist must incur. At night he would attach candles to his straw
hat and tromp into the fields so that he could paint under the
stars. He would go to extreme lengths to 'get it right.' Nothing
could prevent him from the *wrack reeling-in.* The "Breaking
News" was *reeling-in* the soul of the postmaster, the cypress, the
wisdom of the sunflowers.
No longer an official minister, he was a man with a mission. A
man in awe of the natural world, of the 'given,' and his mission
was to deliver it in all its magic and magnificence, to expose the
interior tremors usually neglected and glossed over, to *unhidden*
(the word for 'truth,' or 'knowing,' in Greek is '*aletheia,*' which

means 'the uncovering of beings, un-forgetting. Bringing to *appearance*, then, is the first act of truth) the Universe would be his extended sermon, his offering of grace to mankind.

Modern man is conditioned away from the 'hidden,' from the elemental. He is air-conditioned, conditioned with central heating, conditioned by the anti-septic personal trainer at the gym, by traffic signals and Metro maps, the thruways and freeways, the bus lines and bandwidths, he is hyperdefined and mollified, posturized by gadgetry, he is quantified and standardized into a gutless wonder.

Against this falseness, V marches with his brush brandishing like a gleaming sword — "So much is demanded nowadays that painting seems like a campaign, a military campaign, a battle or a war."[9] A campaign to reclaim the world? And this was before the Enemy of *Being* was bedizened with iPhones, iPods, computers, smartphones, Twitters, Facebooks, — a world of Screen Congregations!

Let's announce it, Loud & Clear – Artists Are The Guardians Of Being! And what, you ask, chiding me, is *Being*. *Being* is that *ground* upon which we mark our days. It is the realm of the possible, the root of all activity, the tributary to the infinite.

If V never fulfilled his early goal of becoming a pastor like his father, perhaps he would take comfort in knowing he paralleled a Rabbinical Adept, as a person who followed in his painting, in

---

[9] Letter 182, *The Letters of Van Gogh*, (Penguin Classics).

his looking — in *the regard* — Rabbi ben Bag Bag's prescription for the Torah – "Turn it and turn it, for everything is in it."
To Glare is to contaminate with presence. It is Fecundity's Offspring.
Would V attempt to ward off glare?
I think not.

in the ground of being

uncovering   foundational seepage

                                                    the bleed through

wrack reeling

                                    underbellying old myths

spo(r)(t)ting scarcity as temptation

drinking cloud

Regard

The regard is the look strapped with the interrogative.
The look propelled by a relentless *gaze-into*.
The *gaze that calls forth*. That lariats the subject.
[Are we initializing raw data?]
[Are we tying the 'beast' of appearance to a hitching post.
Subordination for inspection?]

On hearing music, V said, "I should be watching the musicians
rather than listening." *Busy* with *watching/regarding*. The
"regard," the
"watch" becomes an ontic act – the act of enfolding, a grasp-
in(un)to, a journey to(ward) ://: a bringing to,
en(rapturing)wrapping the essential truth of a subject.
We turn to watch his "watching."
The letters announce V's Visuality:

"The ride into the village was so beautiful. Enormous mossy
roofs of houses, stables, covered sheepfolds, barns. The very
broad-fronted houses here are set among oak trees of a superb
bronze. Tones in the moss of gold-green, in the ground of
reddish or bluish or yellowish dark lilac-grays, tones of
inexpressible purity in the green of the little cornfields, tones of
black in the wet tree trunks, standing out against the golden rain
of swirling, teeming autumn leaves, which hang in loose clumps
– as if they had been blown there, loose and with the light
filtering through them – from the poplars, the limes and the
apple trees." (Letter # 340 to Theo)

The Regard unspools our conditioned, habituated modes of
response. The viewed must be approached denuded of
prejudicial pilings, of all we have been taught — the learned, the
schooled. Being "busy" looking means being in attendance,
paying attention to, — tending, tenderizing. A romance ensues
between the viewer and the seen. The seen is stripped, bared of
the inessential, the store-bought, the artificial, disrobed to pure
scrutiny, bathed in solar glow, intoxicated[10] with the ambrosial
lariat of the imagination, roping the sweetheart, the arousal
between viewer/viewed gains in pitch, in intensity, there is
frisson, development, excitement, as the seer/seen gain
proximity, Joy builds as the revelation of flesh surrenders itself,
there is the agony of admission, the natural, wild resistance to
enjoinment, the effort (and terror) required to bring forth, to
invite surrender, ... from gathering this intimacy, → The
Ecstatic Extraordinary![11]

---

[10] In a similar "intoxication" Nietzsche writes: "But whoever is related to me
in the height of his aspirations will experience *veritable ecstasies* [italics mine]
of learning; for I come from heights that no bird ever reached in its flight, I
know abysses into which no foot ever strayed."

[11] In *The Origin of the Work of Art,* Heidegger says: "The setting-into-work
of truth thrusts up the unfamiliar and extraordinary and at the same time thrusts
down the ordinary and what we believe to be such."

in the temperature of regard

abeyance   concordance

             concatenation

conspicuity

             curl cluster storm warnings

the outward is the inward established

                 retinally keyboarding

light analyzed as supine

             as sufferable

as hirsute invitation   mammalian

concerned about young

intestinally tracking   digestive & courteous

breedpropellingvisualvoracity

discretions tracked

conspicuity

is the orderly of silence.   the legend of

legerdemain.   the breeze that

whisks, ... fades.

event elopements.

partitioned compromise.

bringing forth

the hurl deposits its sweetness in

the red eye of the laudatory

The arts appeal because they are aPPEALing. The museums are crowded for more reasons than simply that people have nothing better to do and feel obligated to satisfy a minimum cultural quotient. Or, as a way to justify trips abroad, to substantiate they are not frivolous. When they share pictures on their iPhones they won't look like total lightweights to friends and families. But there is that other factor — the *appeal,* and that is the artwork calling-in, appealing, claiming attention. Releasing its wild hormones into the atmosphere, vivid because it is vitalistic, magnetizing because it is Feral with Real.

The *appeal* is the call, the mandate, the *alarm to look.* The *claw.*

In all my VG readings, there is much discussion of his troubled character, his torment, his insanity, with very little discussion of his Eurekas, the Rapture his visuals afforded him. If he experienced more depression than the common man, it is equally probable he experienced more ecstasy. In letter #192, he writes Theo: "I am filled with zest and ambition for my job and my work ...." This zest factor, the zing of his enterprise, has been curiously omitted from observation and speculation. Doesn't the question of why a man possesses so much passion and fortitude, such a Love for his calling, command as much attention as why he went insane? Why do pain and insanity tract more commercial cache than joy and effulgence?

Rapture

is the revelation of transport. The gift of ignition. Rapture
entails being Enwrapped. Winding/wounding inside around –
binding to. To perceptually be aswirl with/in — with-in — the
subject. Internal Swirling. Becoming Subject. Fusion. Rapture
self-vacates. Removes the self from where it was, — *transports.*
The practice of this aptitude could undermine the Travel &
Entertainment Industry. But it is not our intent to incite
sedition.[12]

Rapture :*//*: Raptor:
The intense focus of the raptor upon its prey, the *keening* ... the
flight to, the approach, the preparation of claw, the pounce,
entanglement, then – *nutrition.* What concerns us is
"approach," the coupling for engainment –
Pr(ey)ay

---

[12] "That *rapture* was for those who could feel it; for people who could not, it
was non-existent." from Willa Cather's O *Pioneers,* Part four, "The White Mul-
berry Tree," Chapter 6. (Italics mine.)

with rapture this transport

lift   evacuation   leave to go
to (with) → toward
— ward — of
being the ward of the viewed
not in paltry arrest but in transfusion
the arrest of capture captivated by
fusions fertilizing
crossbreeding   plenishment fests   rowdies
the gift of the predatorial wing —
pr(ayer)(ey)dom —
Ingest
prehensile claw

Starry Night

(*after* Van Gogh

stir volupt   virulent voracity fevers
catechism quakes   flush velocity colossus upcharge
calendrical sweep
           coilchurn welt divinity
dervish feints
coalitional chaos fest
manic orb agitators
great chieftain serpentine wallop tongue simoom swap gash –
liquid columbine – trawling indigo mountain waterfall poise
relish of

the village is pocketed, downsized toward the bottom of the
canvas, the yellow lights through the windows signal hearth,
comfort, the village is dwarfed by nature's voluptuous kinetic,
the Ferally Cosmic – the steeple is puny, impecunious, static &
benign, compared to the torrential energy rattling through the
cypress, ... is this a commentary on the religious, championing
true religiosity as being organically cosmic, not approachable by
the man-made makeshifts, the artificially gathered, the
diminutive imitations. Or is this dichotomy artificial, could the
whole starry night be viewed as one vast vitalistic enterprise,
seething energy systems seizing scaling

swapping ferrying universal plasmas, the universe: one mighty
artery occasionally breached, occasionally embellished, always
rotational & decisive →

→

chlorophyllian bleed

Theo as Landscape

Theo was going to see V's paintings. And he needed a break.
Little Vincent (the baby named after his brother) kept him up
nights, his employers were hassling him for expending energy on
the non-remunerative Impressionists, and he missed his brother.
He missed his solidity, ... his fire. It had been a long while since
they had spent time together. Last week when he visited was a
fiasco. An anxiety chamber. The baby was sick, he and Jo were
bickering over finances, he feared for his job, and Vincent's
presence was more of a nuisance than a pleasure. He was sure V
felt intrusive.

He couldn't sell his brother, but he believed in him. Vincent
had a courage he could only marvel at.
He had chosen to paint.

News of Theo's plan to visit served as an internal pump.
Paris had been devastating: Eyeballing the newborn,
experiencing the tensions radiating throughout the family,
empathing the severe stresses Theo was undergoing, all
combined to magnify V's already pronounced sense of
marginality. The glaring hardship he was costing his brother by
requiring subsistence was hurled front and center. Not a
pleasant sight. Assessing himself as anything other than a

burden would be sheer lunacy. But he would make it up to him. He would not betray his brother's confidence in his art. Theo would be rewarded. Many times over.[13]

They dined at Auberge Ravoux, table #5.
They both chose the *Waterzooi De Poissons* (Monkfish and Mussel Stew) to honor their heritage, a dish that could be considered a Northerner's bouillabaisse.

They discussed the Impressionists and V supported T's enthusiasm, but with caveats. Certainly he had profited from their lightened palette, but he needn't let on to Theo his indebtedness, nothing should distract Theo from *his* supremacy. Any artist should be able to profit from his contemporaries, they had to have something to offer, though none of them, other than Seurat, would have his longevity, the enduring Vitriolic Impact.

Having his brother all to himself was wonderful. Theo wasn't equally approving of all his pieces. Theo's judgments showed discernment, though they didn't always align with his own.

They were on their second bottle of Beaujolais. Dessert was Le Tarte Tatin. They were happy together. Celebrating was appropriate.

---

[13] And repay his brother he did. Theo's son, in the 1940s, was valued one of the richest men in the Netherlands.

Unfortunately, there were no brothels in Auvers-sur-Oise as in Arles.

After a brief stroll to settle their meal, they retired to his room. V's best work hung on the walls; he had made every effort to appoint the room attractively. To house Theo in style.

His brother had *trop bu* (overdrank) and practically crashed on the bed. It was to be expected given the stress he was under. V intended to sleep on the couch. He had made the bed look comfortable and inviting. He helped Theo unclothe. When he slipped off Theo's underwear – *he froze.* "Darling" was the only way he could phrase it: — alabaster, pink, aqua-veined, black pubic hairs burbling, sprouting in a gurgle-tangle from the pallid belly, sloping to clash with the chaotic pitch pubic-bramble, the belly and thatch demarcated like opposing chess pieces, and reclining on its side was the 'darling,' serene in its stable, the miniature boulders tucked below, cozily complaisant, secure with puissance, ... Theo turned and the darling moved to its other side, ... V studied the composition, the elemental contrariety, the shivering chiaroscuro, the subtle hues cast across the belly, the sable cushiness of the pubes, and the darling so perfectly shaped, so sculptural, so scented ....

hands holding a bowl

Nuenen, 1885
Black chalk, 8¼ x 13¾ inches
Van Gogh Museum, Amsterdam

curvatures   a curling collection

a coil hive

bowl → the stir thing

, the torso winding,

winding *toward*

, curves compiling

, a point of view

bowl → a gatherer, … gather-*ing*

, souping intimacies (hands, fingers,

nails, spoon, bowl, …

wood, flesh, cloth, … rounding,

roundup, a sloop

grouping, a reconnoiter)

accrual   crewelwork

, occurring

work accruing in the lapping occur-stir

Peasant on Fire

(*from* Van Gogh's *Patience Escalier*

seed   peasant soil-sprout

earth-ejaculate

stationed by blue wind winging migratory wheat land

in: coruscant-carve

    cretaceous-beget

swallow: the errant gust of lapidarian permissiveness

reading the 'look': a question?

            a window into landscape?

Peer-Less

→ VG paints a look, a peer, that vanishes. that disclaims intention. en-visionment Un-throned. a face so sturdily *there* that it disappears. so assuredly dense that it dissimilates into peripatetic grief, a "Pair of Boots" scything pigment fields, sturdy studs cleating root.

conveying this paradox — face/not face — poses the painting as koan, the paradox mel(t)(d)ing into compositionally assimilative fields.

portraits by van Dyck, Franz Hals, or Rembrandt, express personality, the "peasant" expresses transparency. it collapses into the infinite.

seen also:

a congregation in disguise. face as interim plane where ferality gathers, where cypress & olive trees, boots, chair, sunflower, crow, portrait, pigment, sower, sheaf & breeze, bunch into form, to disperse when witness sunders, peeling from formula, each element grappling with its separateness, their varied sentiments, trembling

in the loft
of liquid
decibel

.

Tree Roots and Trunks

(*after* Van Gogh

dive — *davening* — down

                              reticular splurge

congressional probe

churl-holler

the electromagnetic brook affair

ushering electromagnetic sweep filtrative hygiene pour

— ... density eclipse   hover

        that time – NoW

                        pre-storm:

ga(i)ted marshaling

stillness avalanche

quartering earth's erogenous supplicity

Wheatfield with Crows

breakage/repair   ascensional whorls   roots uplifting
wheat, — winging
exhalations

                              *

spinning triadic imagery:
     panoramic medley:

Tree Roots/Wheatfield with Crows/brook storm, — ricocheting
imagery, mashed to a vortex of clashing incendiaries, ... brook
behaving as apex, as intensity chute, — brook   crow   tree   root
wheat   sky   cloud   storm — brook pre(c)luding storm,
twitching darkness, resembling the bucking chute before the gate
opens, bull & bull rider stalled, staffed, drenched in suspension,
a tension rubberized, ... → stretched   →   →
bull bolts   roots sprout from crow wings dunk-tangle
fingering stream uteral froth fidget tunnelings the vaulted wheat
gardens the cherished incipience incandescent vaginal galleries

Was painting compensation for Vincent? Is it fatuous to speak
of 'compensation' for enormous deprivations? Could Vincent
find Love in Paint? Would it ever serve
as a Home?

Cezanne

smock blue

(on blue smock in Cezanne's
The Card Players, 1890–1892)

blue loam roaming run rivulet roar cascades Crashing carom
terraplane blues

the casual smock   protect   to un-encumber activity   so much
depends
smock-wrap portrait warps
a ruminant gnarling
paint slurps

rhapsody in blue
blue train
kind of blue
blue moon
blue moon of kentucky
blues at sunset
blues festival
sky blue
sea blue
blue jeans
blue collar
blue guitar
blue horse 11
blue smock

larval folds   sussurant runes   rum volleys

sinking into blue   vast swallow   swelter

to extract the smock, & only that, from the canvas, to study
smock, as landscape, as fleshscape, facescape, as narrative –
platoons carillons   pastorals cathedrals dreamcurrents lion
manes   viper bellies   ravine bushwhackings   langorous
Mediterranean   alpine fisheries   sequestrian runes   primary
considerations   running as gravitational bluff   commentary as
tonal bunchings   lagoon roundups   knave festoons   keynote
speeches   necklace   splash pasterns   sinew stations   huddle …

                                                    h

                                                       u

r   d

le

wildlife preserve ... growth: is growth wild by definition? is
decline? does decline decline wildly? what is stasis?

announcing non-preservable/reservable wildlife
wild burning wild

imbibing smock   blue intoxicant   to know a color, a smock, ...
intimately [an intention to *knowing* intimately {knowing
intimately, lappings at/with the unknowing, ... burblings,
provocations, — *unearths*}]

Professor Emeritus **Blue Smock**
the smock instructs: assess the course differential between
'yellow smock instruction,' & 'blue smock instruction'
color capaciousness
the narrative of color tonalities, chaptering the color spectrum,
page-turning densities
"color ... becoming the expression of distance"
the plot is motion
trestles threshing
trespass in obdurate credulity
exhumation

THE CARD PLAYERS   Paul Cezanne, French/Oil on canvas, early 1890s

TREES AMONG ROCKS   Paul Cezanne, watercolor and graphite, c1890

Trees among Rocks

(*after* Cezanne

rockabilly   leg through

            (the middle rock, horse from sideview, head on
rump, the leg going through — the horse's, ...
x-ray rock – skeletal combustions, paleolithic musing: art first
appears on rock, rock, — primary witness)

jamb   enjambment
trees = verticals   lines engineering →   root line   top to
bottom   upon paper   papering
peppering
through-ways / through rocks   upon paper
                         *** trees almsgiving

rocks   ///
interse(xuals)ctionals   pillars
(to hold (held   (- columnary   , columnizing   anointments
ghost mingles,
tingling

                                    support
altar spread   altering with cognition   with beatific vacuum
with perspirational vicinity
enlivening consanguineous consortium

shapes   shape-speaking
elucidating
each twig an incident
every rock a branch

rocks

rock — scape

scape — land

word – rock   land – word

word-scape

rockland wordscape

wordscaping rockland

scar inscape escarpment larking

rocks   brilliantine

shingling

rock   glaze foundries

earth's pastor   , fertility frocks

rock beggary

supplications

wind-winds winding

sends rock-scent   lifting ...

word,

the hunts-

man

Picasso

did picasso strum?

(after "Picasso: Guitars 1912–1914," at MoMA

I don't think so. An obligatory google search popped-up a
teacher in Indiana who said Picasso did play musical
instruments because he wanted to know how things work. But,
that's from a teacher in Indiana. One can discern how a guitar
works without strumming one. Was he curious? Sure. That's
why he drew so many guitars. Did he have a guitar? Sure.
There was a photograph of one in his studio. So, if he liked
wine & women, why not song? Can you picture him in his
studio, with those onyx eyes, decked out in the Breton Striped T-
shirt he made famous, surrounded by a cadre of dazzlingly
beautiful women, back-dropped by brilliant canvases, sitting on
an old wooden stool belting out Spanish sea songs. Or perhaps
he fired a series of rasquedos from a flamenco guitar, barked for
dancers, & launched into Andalusian wail. All this is possible.
But it didn't happen. What happened is he played the guitar —
Visually. Compositionally. He eye-strummed, retinally fingered,
optic-nerved. He created 4-string guitars, with frets made of
strings, with succulently curved bodies, with wood made of flesh,
genitalia-glazed tuning machines, vaginally inviting sound holes.
Guitar = Seduction.
But Picasso could not choose to Strum over Painting & Drawing.
Did he ever place a guitar upon his lap? Probably. Did his
fingers ever come into contact with a string? Probably. But
mostly he studied. Looked long & hard at the grain, the shape

of the bridge, how it flushed against the soundboard, ran his hand over the curves, stroked up & down the rounded underside of the neck.

He flirted with the idea of playing the guitar until Sabicas. While drinking with two women from a bottle of Bordeaux in the Rose Café, a non-imposing man sat down at a chair near the piano, positioned the microphone before his guitar, and began playing "Ritmos de Paraguay." Picasso listened. & listened. He didn't respond to his friends. He didn't drink. He listened. Never again did he flirt with the idea of playing the guitar. No one could do with the brush what he, Picasso, could. Why would he jeopardize his dominance with a dalliance, a domain where he'd clearly play an inferior role. He enjoyed prestige. The ability to seduce. To have, to do, *whatever* he wished. That power didn't come from being second rate.

Picasso sucked his thumb. This little-known fact does not bring us closer to answering the question of whether or not he strummed. But it does help explain his success with women far his junior. Wealth, power, celebrity-hood, could all lose their appeal for persons of substance. A powerful man, on the other hand, writhing amid a tangle of vulnerabilities, in need of nourishment, of maternality, could attract. Could make a woman feel needed. Important. Even powerful. Picasso was scrupulous: — he only sucked his left thumb; he ensured it never became too raw; & only exposed his thumb-sucking to women he felt he could trust. Women so flattered to be admitted to his inner kingdom that they would never dream of betrayal.

There isn't one painting of a thumb-sucker.

Joan Mitchell

story phosphorous

(tales from Joan Mitchell

I didn't get it. At first. Walking into the gallery, her paintings,
... why would she "hit me between the eyes." I rotated , ...
stalled, ... , saw just another abstract artist, — color, Pollock-
like swipes & slashes, ... so? I had never been ill-advised by
Clayton Eshleman before, his saying she'd "hit me between the
eyes" was strong, I needed to consider, to slow down, to gear-
shift, to retread, why should recognition be immediate, ... in the
slowing, the quieting, the paintings began to emerge, to talk, the
diptychs clutched into motion, the walls receded,
color/configuration enlarging ... – shall we dance.
Dance is movement, sprays of Lilliput, disorder saddling, the
algae tentative but not without purpose, the cradle in its rock
not without its billy,
... persuasion chances, courts co-ordinates, — narrative,
painting as narrative, abstraction as narrative, how that which
does not represent represents. Representation behaving as a
form of repute morphs into the Recognition Factor. Peek-a-boo,
I see You ...
Nefertiti & the anxiety of reign.
Did you move to Vetheuil, Joan, to imbibe Monet? Was it
comforting living close to one of the artists you admired most?
The road to proximity road. Monet's colors bleeding into
yours. Blood diptych. Vesseling(')s dispatch. Nuclei
emancipated.

Monet as neighbor – residence/ambiance diptych. Persuasion power-barreling, …. plumb lines no longer faulty, but leaderly, underwritten in sidereal sublimity, squalls from the North country, the pitiable & the impoverished bleed-out, the paint brush controlling a bleed- out? the paint brush bleeding into a bleed-out? the nature of control & what is blood-worthy, … taste maximizes closer to the bone, blood-lush, applies to walls & floors as well as canvas, is paint seeking the plasma of blood, to stir circulation, is paint the canvas's plasma, pumping from the painter's heart?

the text, the written, can travel with/through the mouth, is vibrant with portability, syntax-scintillative, … the painting travels only by being seen, in the being seen, is there to be s(c)e(ne)en, there, upon the wall, rarely on the floor or the ceiling, the wall & the painting, the painting on the wall, a stab at remark, to achieve remarkability, traveling *to* the remarkable, a remarkable painting attracts a remarkable number of people, people traveling to the remarkable painting remark upon the remarkable, provisional or not, at some level functions the Stun Factor, do the people come to be stunned? is stunning a human need?

Those in the gallery with me, are they receiving stories? Do our stories collaborate, overlap, intersect, dispute?

Can I agree with the catalogue that the canvas *Then, Last Time* "expresses Mitchell's quest to simultaneously acknowledge & dismiss time by pushing her abstraction to a less conscious level…?" That *Then, Last Time,* might suggest Mitchell's life was now in jeopardy & her deep-felt commitment to & lifelong love of painting was threatened?"[14]

Or do I view the painting as a grappling, two titan arachnids duking it out above an efflorescing periwinkle vortex, a plume coagulative brewing Orphic density flares, considerations trans-personal, time-evaporative, the spume of artistic privilege vesseling Ceremonial Tug, partaking in Cosmic Concussion, the report striking without saying, narratives accumulating in lullaby coax, lollapalooza loam, ...

what is the narrative of creek, of river, of tree, ... of stone, moss, bridge, ... of spire, ... of fire, ...

can you tell?

---

[14] In the 1980s Mitchell was diagnosed with cancer & also underwent a serious hip-replacement surgery that left her mobility impaired. "Mitchell became painfully aware of her own mortality ...."

the road to proximity road

nearing   coming upon

closing toward/in   → clearing

.....

                     a spun affluence

              influential adjacencies

        corded influences

accordion wind

ings   warded, tende(re)d

attentiveness   considerations   scrutiny

avowals

plantings rendered

planted

redresses overturned

capsized

Michael Dominick

Michael Dominick's painting with Molten Iron smote me.
The Upcharge of Earthly Essentials to Canvas impressed me as
Hinge Devotional.

painting in the mold of fire

(*from* Michael Dominick

"molten iron as paint" as leap,   tortured twist,

...

scorch utterance

in the valley of ... where eagle wing & leviathan lash hibernate
across the blades of god, — god, (lost & found), , , fire &
the upholstery of groin, ,

diatribe
ductility

— New Jersey → the New Mount Etna —

tell me of Hephaestus   Vulcan   Ogoun   Apris   Agnis
Xiuhtecuhtli &
Dominick
of the forge   the slash
— *magnum lush syrup serrying collusional goop gurgling in*
   reams of quagmire rent ...
   formation ://: obsolescence
   lowland epiphanic moan

gesture: from commotion → configuration
iron, ore, coke, limestone, — carbon monoxide gas →
oxygen reductivity → lesion chemistries

formulation: → editing
the edited paradiddling giddy escape furlough dispatch surefires
hatch hilarious in sneak cocoons

creation as rupture   the symphony of vast   aperture →
aparting → opportunities

excision   surmise,   — surprise
  solubility lexicons
    skirmish texts

congruence after the table is eaten

familiarity :://: absence

Q: Where is memory in the cauldron of fire?

A: Where isn't it.

levitational admix spray longitude

Heller: At The Brasserie Julien, I challenged your statement that "each drawing bears the marks of the controlled chaos that brought it into existence" by asking:

"What is the value of displaying/submitting "chaos" — controlled or otherwise? We have only to watch a storm, a river." & you fast forwarded to your radiator exhibits & the "tradition of ready-made," correctly pointing out how you have extended/expanded that tradition by presenting the object in integral enactment, performing "their original function." The museum goers view the steam sprouting from the radiator, they feel its warmth, they can experience the radiator in a way they have never experienced a radiator before. In your words, "they'll never forget this."

To which I now say, well & good. I mean, no one pisses in Duchamp's urinal. Although that's a cool idea, hey, why don't I install a couple walls of fully working urinals, recontextualize the Men's room so that it is seen as Art. This would be, I think, an extension of the readymade; for now, not only would the object, the Urinal, be recontextualized, so would the museum goer, and the "man in the men's room," because those two men have now become a third, an art object enacting Urinal Utilitarianism. *Art News* will bill me as the first great Piss Artist! Title of *The New York Times* Review: "A Real Pisser!"

A little fun, yes?

Michael: "Hysterical!"

painting in the lissom like combustible jeté

lissom

                    lissom-ness

      crux cuillery

                              crewel

the contemplation of temperature

temperature as geography

tensility: a temperature *in remark*

ladle with arch   the ballerina foot

the ballerina bosom   arch as

applied to utensil   bosom as

applied to fustian disarray

combustibility tenebrous in the mold of fire

iron species the earth   praxis &

mantis   ferrum

                    (fer-ality

fer – til   *tillity*

temerity weighs indicative carries less flavor regulates without
stern

Q: Isn't "mold" in your title anti-hinge as it suggests a
formalization, a circumspection?

A: Is there anything formalized or circumspect about fire?

combustion fricative but never careless

scrub foundry farfara limpidity

ask of your father:
why is there color?

when he answers:
what color is rain

hug him

percussive pant molt hybridity complex

beat sets a pattern
                    (serial-izes
beat releases pattern

occipital rose
              ris-ing
                risible
                visible
                            ri-sion ://: vi-sion
    viscosity

compromise a release from compound vision

when visionaries melt they spray

warriors arose who understood the integrity of the blade
such that
only blood will do

pulsation Little Walter "Mellow Down Easy" molt foundry burn
properties blister hip jump fracas my babe I'll eat your earlobe
out shake easy mold gelid whippy wiggle omnibus bullseye

caucus cancel inconsiderables uprise

glamour: Vogue International

no, ...

> *Kiss My Action!*

glamour is

wallop juju shrink concinnitous
lissom lean-to tributarial
perilous disarray upcharge

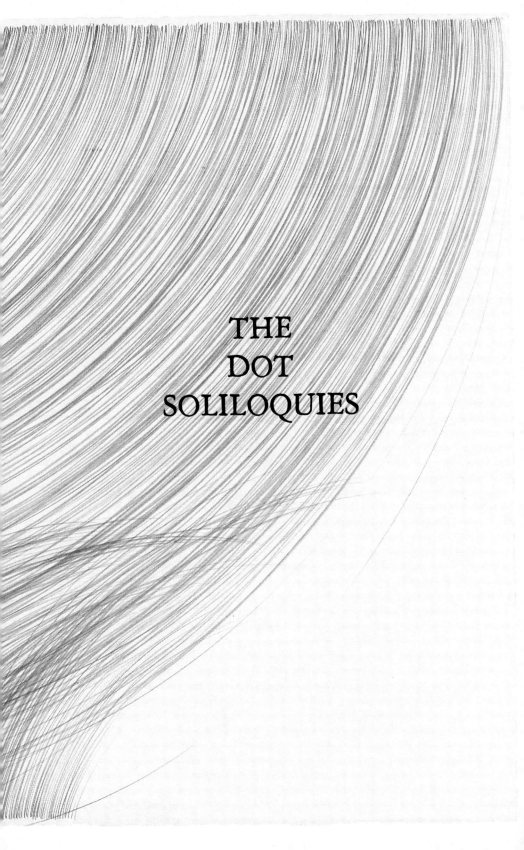

THE
DOT
SOLILOQUIES

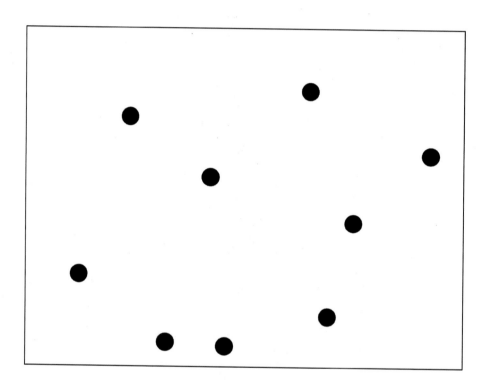

WRACK LARIAT

The Dot Soliloquies

were provoked by a visit to the artist/publisher Kurt Devrese in Ghent, Belgium. The dancer Victoria Ganim and I were wrapping up a two-week Van Gogh pilgrimage. We had made plans to meet with Kurt on our way to Auvers-sur-Oise, VG's final resting place.

Kurt opened the door and we were friends. When we went upstairs to visit his studio, he opened a fat notebook writhing in Dots. I flipped through them, abuzz, and, while walking downstairs, said: "with dots."

And so, — The Dot Soliloquies.[15]

---

[15] The Dot Soliloquies are termed a Hinge Treatment.

Cogitation Dot: A Prolegomena

point   a designation   a brief a
pause a   period.   .periodicity
a dot is perspectival & rarely remorses. star is a pin-sized dot.
tinier than the lowliest coin.
the dot is the ballerina of distance
dot is flattering punctuation favoring formation is a formation
function flows formatively ferments both breakage & repair
a dot is sagacious placed properly is a seasonal spilling. is a
perplexity bribe

.... 	...	::	.....

placing dots is a spec-*ial*-ity   ..   dots proscribe are proscriptive
control fly-away laundry & promote hierarchy.. dots prohibit
outlawry & stimulate the economy. nations are fond of dots.
so are dogs. dog noses are replete with dots...   ...... dots are
prehensile & fawn. they live in trees & shrubbery. chimneys &
wallets. they are flirtatious & have a mind of their own. they
avoid gimmickry. they munch on vacillation & digest systems
analysis.

crow — the black dot on the green lawn of grammatical vacuity

dots are punchy perk ferric febrile. not feeble.
dots are absent of putridity. are affirmative. non-totalitarian.
strict yet conductive. dots don't talk back. but may be seen as
squeaky. not squeaky as squeaky clean but squeaky.

what does it mean to say that someone is full of dot.

paintings attract dots: Seurat. Signac.
dot plays a major role in color therapy
... .
dot is a to is a do is Phoenician & Soho is od & ot is
t   o   d & dot
is integral to assembly is a . in the assembly process

to be a dot is to be both conspicuous & benign. is to be both
gatekeeper & emancipator. is to be a multiplier & a time value
is to be
a
point

with dot this emancipation

striped regimental   assembled
            skewered
        a confederacy

           spunked

    o-   m-   o-
from f- r-   a-   i-

        t-
n   striking
spurred to pluration
        supple
suppling
        muscle-ing
  solar crepes
zesting in non-clumpery
  calandering rotational rigour
    outriggery

collapse
an in-surge
a with draw-in
proximity
cobbling

with dot this circumference

the *ground* of *being* a dot is
round surround
this round surround
                              this
bound round surround ground
sound   sonic like circumferential
dot   outline as both a
forecast & a temperature
a soliloquy in dialogue
borderlines swell self-identifiaby
dot blistering coruscant curiosity coinage
struggling with
fate
binding

<< alternate >>

with dot this circumference

this round surround

         this

bound round surround ground

sound   sonic like circumferential

dot   outlines both a

forecast & a temperature

a soliloquy in dialogue

borderlines swell self-identifiability

dot blistering curuscant curiosity coinage coruscate?

struggling with

fate

binding

> the *ground*
> of *being* a
> dot is
> round
> surround

smelling dot

an adventure
in inhalation

dot ..like contagious entropy

.

arachnid floral   . whirring
canister cupolas   lesion ice

      glut guttering
frantic flummeries swollen with bruise   .
with epoxy quilted from exotic ancestral acids splurging
slurp.anatomical misgivings.buckshot shorn of firepower ..
errant.mischievious .. tasting god as cherry vanilla
    embellishing a maundering parousia
. ...
.. ..
.. ..
    ..

               ..

born under the trapezius of a malevolent delta improvisatory
crossfires ignite wings of noncentering aporias careening
clutchless vertiginous zithers asphyxiating blooms burst like
calamitous blame souping in aphotic scalps committed to
training mystical vandalism
.
  . ....
.   .
.
.   .   . .
   .
  .

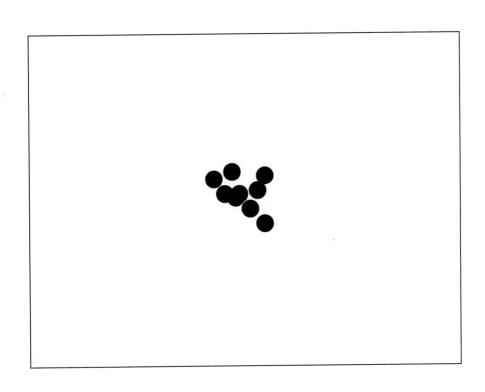

dot like equipoisal sled

                      fillip

poise

                                    curvature

      glee

                              bounce

                         shuffle

load

          branch baron

[poise fillip glee curvature

bounce shuffle branch load baron]

dot like lugubrious plot

stoppage. gap. stopgap. a precedent that barks. an
antecedent that br(e)ak(e)s. an earned license. bold whole roll.
pointed pin. pine. to pine as a dot. the pining dot travels to
Nashville. dressed as a country singer. dot chromatics.
uppage. wattage. dot as a circling surrender. a surrendering
circle. a point that points. a placement that bargains. an
appointment. a blot on the infinity plot. a plot to blot. to
arrest. to take over. a makeover. an abrupt. an abutment.
an ----------- in.sin.u.ation. situating in. *in situ.* dots don't
loiter. or litter. a littering dot would be a freak. freaks require
special care. freak care units. dots are mobile & love
exchange. thrive on shift & glide. groupings & disbursements.
on insertions & perspicuities. perspicacities & punctuation.
punch. push. press. pre. cision. intolerant of persiflage.
dots shape. establish. contribute to empires. while umpiring
empires. dots are territorial yet civilized. tend to spot a spot to
plot. dots rarely say hello. nor do they slumber. to slumber as
a dot is to mislead.
to betray diligence.
to court insouciance.
no. dots are enspherically virile. are preferential. preferring to
bathe in the suds of the emphatic. while maintaining
cognizance. — of drift.   .   ...
.. ..

.

.

dot like omnicropping utensil

                                ::.or.the song of the spherically
insistent.::
service.   ... center
        service center
service doesn't require a center. to be
central. balance. requires balance. an articulating poise. (:)
[.]
equi-distant. point - poise.   posing.
dimension. measurement.   a dot details
distance. embraces arbitration.
                          plagiarism
is not service. it is a not. a rebuke. a conscience spill. the
majority of writing is plagiarism. is inauthentic. spills from the
unoriginal self. is contaminated with corrosive. the dot
performs. dutifully. doesnt pretend. to be other. than what
it is. placing a dot serves. intends. sets off. distinguishes.
                      putting
a dot here. instead of there.   the integrity of placement.
putting here putting there. here a dot there a dot. everywhere
a dot dot. buckshot dot. a universe of dots. is more dottified.
dots dont search for signature. they indicate.
point. spherically
insist   offer
spherical insistence.

dot like omnidripping crop

(dripping key of F

                              is

crop happy.   field worthy.   flotationally flush.   fulsome.
fructuous.

fulgurous .:::: ... :::::::::::::: :::::::: ....:::::::::::::   foliate
fortified with amplicative varietals flushforming fricative frisson
coinage evergreen fulmination fusioning fructation funds
forming

fulgent
fornicatory
ferrying infamous ferric fare
famous for
fermata

dot like omnicropping drip

.   .   .
.   .
.   .   .
.   .   .
.   .   .
.   .
.   .
.   .
.   .   .
.   .   .
.   .   .
.   .
.
.   .   .
.
.   .
         .
.   .   .
.   .   .
.   .
.   .   .
.   .

         .
         .
         .
         .
         .
           .
         .

.
.
.

.
.
.
.
.
.
.
.
.
.
.

omnicropping like prestidigitating dot

fructuous flow confluence flews bearing voluptuous force field
flamboyance
omnipresence oscillating auscultate persuasion   seething
unheards   transmigrational entooling   placing point
punctuation pours
purposefully predatorily predicate   predated by   raining like
dots
identifying dot grain   flooding formula presumptions
peccadilloes
folding furling with scrumptious crop-glow   glamorous
gallimaufry
installing concussive concurrency
short of collateral
rabbits
dotting
from dot
trade dot

dot like propositional shrub (alternate take)

em

theor

lean

assert

gauge

posture

measure

water root

.   .

foundation

[foundation water root posture measurement gauge

lean assert theorem]

dot like composition com

.com.com.com.com.comcom..com
   com.com.com.   .com.com.com.e.ly
.com e ly   .come.ly   .comely .comelycom
comely comely   .. .   com com com .
.com.com   .   comb   comb.com   comb.e.com
combecom   .com   comecombecome
become.com   combecomecombcom
   comb.com   come come.com come
comecome calm   calm.com   comb calm
   come.calm   comcom   calm
.   .   ..   comecomecomecomecom
comcomcomcomcomecom
comcalmbecome   comecomebecomecum
cum cum cum   cumcumcum.cum   cum..cum
 comebecomecombcum comb cum cumcombcomecombcom
combcum   cumcom   cum.com
com.cum   comecumcome
c   a   l   m
cumcomcome up comb up   comeup.com
upcomupcombcombcom.com
         comeup.calm
         calm.comeup

comeupcalmcalmcomeupcalmcomcalmbecomeupbecomecumbec
omecalm
calmcalmcalmcalmcomcomcomcumcumcombcomeupbecome

comeuppance

.com

becomecomeuppance.com

.comcomcom

in the proposal of dot

to dot. matrimonial intent. ring. plans. plans ceremonies
occasions routine ritual cake icing ruckus. rickrack. rickety.
ricochet. the value is in emerging markets. in emergingweds.
when dots wed. whats the spread. dot to dot is good to got.
go. dots dance the circle. circling. do the circlebreak. have
boundaries. advantageous boundaries. prevents crossovers.
spills. corruptions. contagions. dilutions. distilments.
disillusions. prevents pouring into one another. comfort
circumference. non-circumstantial. encasement. case. just in
case. unknown dangers. protect. to protect. protecting
valuables. valuables encased. just. in case. protect valuables.
casement protects. non-boundaried lovers unprotected. are not
spheres. a sphere is a whole. a wholeness. wholeness is
wholesome. wholesomely whole. o.o.o.o.ooooooooo unwhole
lovers often seek to annihilate themselves. to exterminate
themselves in the beloved. seek to pour out. get rid of
themselves. through the other. by means of. the other.
organisms that can penetrate.or. accept penetration are game to
this. interpenetratives awake with ambition. what sort of
organism seeks. to annul itself. the organism with rift
condition. not drift. but rift. rent. wracked. damned to
diffuse. dumb with toward. rife with other. envy the dot. the
dot in its drift to dot. elegant predisposition. to touch another
dot. be close to. near. to place not pierce. pulsation. not
plumbing. alongside. structurally intact. adjoining embrace.
endurable.

in the dark of dot

perturbation, ...   pout
      ponder
      ous
      ing
blot, ...   downsink
pulleying below   (explore the verticality
to/of Suffer) (list the steps in ladder)
descent tug   .   pulls   shroudshifting
    spreadloaves   spearhuddles
:::: ascent leavens empyrean
bound upward   lift
aspire   inspire:::
yet in this gloom
this quilled melancholia —
submerg(ence)ing
enveloping
plunge
without invitation

in the outing of dot

outlaw   lawout   outlying   lying-in-wait
                                                  lawless
                                                  recreation
                                                  reckless
border skirting   bundling trespass
                                                          bumbling enterprise
out confronting dot   cur on the cusp
                                       catastrophe curse
                                       aromatic blinks

stunts
performed in magnificence draws

                                        derring-do Draconian dart
dusting the parliament
flux flexing flexions ungirdle baronial hurdle bruisers rouse-kick-
wallop-spank-whacking the splendiferous flying peppermint
duck dancers creaming strudel dripping Egyptian mascara
scouting reluctance in testimonial pin cushions prickling dot-out
with doubt with forethought afterthought consideration &
compromise dot undeterred hedonistic & rambunctious
commingles with scallion hoppers a.m. uppers spear plungers
dungaree rippers vaseline dippers gin drenched string benders
ferries wheeling contagious circulating merriment wielders
warrior wizards promulgating the overlooked field of anarchistic

finance espousing the fecundity of loot the obsolescence of
privilege the might of delirial surplus the meat of a damaged
ethics careening custodial periphery swathes determined to
succor those overlooked in the gather — a gather gather(s)ing —
a convoy of sloops sarabanding the perilous ocean slopes
dithering in binary miasma trunneling trench trammel pith
freighting feral flirtations febrile flings flung the vast pilgrimage
scrimmage onlookers caretakers screen-gazers the generally
stupefied the unshapely shrivelized testify proclaim orate put the
light on those standing outside the portal the demon abiding
banished hysterical steppenwolves sizzling through gated gravity
burning the clench-drivers the quantification obsessors cindering
the well established the comfortable the overly ambitious the
self-righteous the zealously sterile the well seated yet poorly
assembled identifying remorse as the
immobilized-considered

in the sonic of dot

sanguinity

        no surplus
        moisture

perpetual rock
a nation of reassurances

sound of the winging gull
the rock

Ode on a Dot

(after Keats's "Ode on a Grecian Urn"

Thou yet unblemished point of quiescence,
Thou tribal–child of Stillness and wise Pause,
Sylvan grammarian, who wouldst thus enhance
A turbulent world more smartly than our noise:
What sharp-rimmed form lurks about thy poise
Of octagons or commas or both,
On Broadway or the dales of Collider?
What sales or mass sprint these? What profits froth?
What mad stoppage? What intent to upbraid?
What marks and values? What crazed sequences?

and this,
your intercessional bloom

· · · ·

in the verge of dots to be

(*after* Emily Dickinson's "As if the Sea should part"

involucrum loosing   rattling craters
of canister moss
breakage & repair &
reproduction

a surcease glide
in the throes of an incunabula drift
priming periodicity with pinnings
dots locust swarming — Spray

LINDA LYNCH

In my long search for a cover
artist, Eve Aschheim suggested
I check out Linda Lynch.
Her work ripped through me.
Our Intercourses are a
wellspring in Hinge
Exploration.

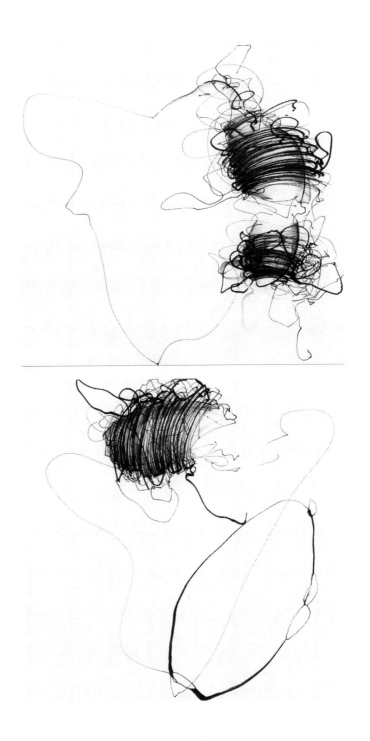

with

(*for* Linda Lynch

line(s), ...
        circling
            circulating
     in circulation ...
            (en-circled-ness
circuitry
de-encrustat(ion)ing
gestation

lean   line lineament ligament ligature littoral ellipses roil
limblong-ing ... — look-lurch — lunge-burst — — lurch
roaming
loam roam   —
         (foam motets
         (borealis broth
              (((gloaming

register gesture
   gesticulastic
gesticula-ting
swirl swizzle storm succu-bus liturgical seductivity warps

sway   sweep

       sweep seepage

seepage sweeping

bowl arachnid spool thread

(*hinging* Linda Lynch's "large empty drawing"

shape contour
             geometrical mist
cymbals terraced imbricative pools
shoals   ((slope*-filings
emblazoned disci
saucers sorcering
bearing: sage
         assuage

the dreams you wish for

the dreams you repent

spooling evocations

invitations harnessed to:

scent discriminatories   lapidarian beguilement

roaming perpetual quiver

~

lapping Cezanne's "Rocks at L'Estaque"

are rocks ever far from the sea?

are rocks the sea's speech?

hopscotching infinity pools wand buttercup locket clasp

cognition recycling yokes the lob-to in anachronistic sidle

emptiness: replete reconciliation

alabaster quoting bronze

*Slope invites Slide. Slide initializes Slippage. Thrones slooping
in Ascensional Unrest spool threads of Uploading Buoyancies.

empty drawings

(*hinging* to Linda Lynch's "empty drawings)

I

tantamounts   talk
    committee

                                [bracket orphans
hesitancies
lush audibility

III

plus   flush
   subtraction
r   e   m   a .i   n   s

III

drawing empty: drawing out, withdrawal
                        , extrude

empty drawing: a pull in(halation), an invitation
                pulley-ing
muffled lace

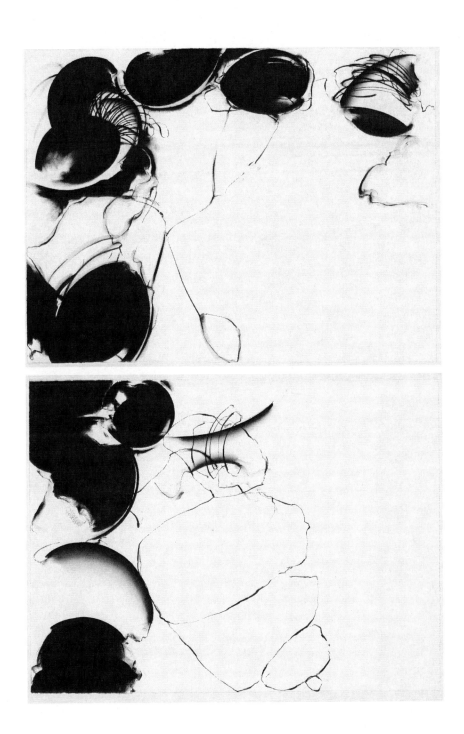

WRACK LARIAT

from the encroaching velocity of drip

(*with* Linda Lynch, jpg, Sept. 2, 2013

gathering(s)
tears cube   atmospheric collation
screens secede
storm protection void
liability: the hiatus

      — smoldering barelys boulder —

fumaroles lace-patted
a heart
gone
vacuum

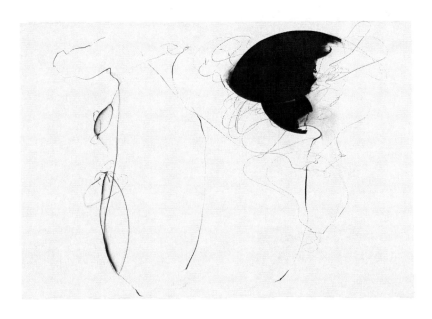

pulmonic lilt

laity

L   U   N   G

fibrillate squall

palpitant filigree

bellows loquacity

                  : tendril crawl

                     crawl: first oasis

fustian fusion foster → *feed*

     — the overdue acquitted

     — turbulence a determination, a decision

skulking overtures inlaid with exquisite undergrowth

keeping apace the audience diminishes

the upturned discharges the respectable

.   .   .

sculling the perimeters → *exhal*

ations

furtive

unclaimable

Bone Springs Rain Grass

(*from* the cover art

mesmeric swirl

        tanta – li – za –tion

marrow leaps   lentil blossoms

      deracinated cylinders luff laden

zi

  g

    g

  u

      r

       at

         sh

         i

       m

          m

        y

Lusitano Meadow

ing

lambent

swells

Bone   Grass

dervish gurge ramp twists fuselage fracas bombinant concavity

the net sum

or

arrays of dispersal

momentum mistaken for direction

for a fib teleology

the root traffics both ways

Rain

precipitation   precipi-tate

          bathe

       personality puddles

burl   broth   frisée burble

    chewy   chime-hustle

cluster frame smithereens garden

         tumbling falcon shuffle

        ordinance frolic

            [can plenishment achieve regainment?

           regainment: the aforementioned

rubbing hide to matriculate

        smothered canopies

aperture pincers moisture-thresh

footnote

a fugitive

mnemonic

Springs

pull   pulled upon

      sought-burgeon

       through-ing

        extru

         de

        extr

        act

      traction

       ex

      traction

    pull :// : beckon

the plea snarling in tumbleweed

cycling a cosmic meander

an agitation born of strata

dredged to the drawn-to

the pull/the tug/the tag-along

the earth lusts for innuendo

for an oblong charisma

for the patchiness

of a

remote

allure

in the dark hour of forlorn this

pause, ... cessation,

celery   caesura   compleat

dirigibles landmarked & crusty concede crustacean failure, aboriginal

diffidence,

eminent domain

remorse is alabaster

          alphabetical convulsion

        spur parades

forlorn, ... mood gentian

melancholy, ... melting iris

from cartoons of an aberrant cartography

, maroon dismissal

masquerades torpedo miscreants & frauds

fallow leers the land

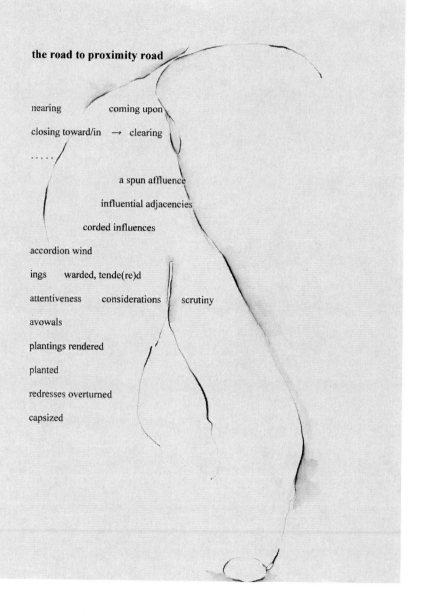

the road to proximity road

nearing   coming upon

closing toward/in → clearing

. . . . .

a spun affluence

influential adjacencies

corded influences

accordion wind

ings   warded, tende(re)d

attentiveness   considerations   scrutiny

avowals

plantings rendered

planted

redresses overturned

capsized

in the wellsprings of aperture

this fraught, ...
interstitial peril   tremor-quirk
quickening piles diffluence, upheaval
in the open-ing

                              — pal pi tate

the let-go   the give-to   the surren-der

how much of

opening

is succumb?

   col-or-ing?

spore   pore   pour

por-ous

a continuation of event planning shellacked to a more
astonishing basis

# of if as in pertaining to *aperture*

crease   cynosure   co-ordinates

appertain

the *ap-pertain-ing*

appertaining to

house arrest invites stir

countdowns fortify collapse

reflex-based embarkations generally

sink

      while

instinctual inceptions dazzle (more

often than not)

fretting the peripheries seldom pays when at rock bottom there

is rock

of if as in pertaining to *appurtenance*

associate   adjunct   prop   proposal   proposition

   appropriate   apportion   access-or-ize

aperture

opportune   option   optimal

            app-e-tite

appetitively   *to*

cynosure curational rotations wellspring curvatures

rampant with boll weevil wrapped in the glutinous sleeve of

ubiquity the

outcome seldom matches the expectation

apropros   apparently   sacrosanct   situational

apperception

applause

audit

ought to be

de-railings coax the openings near to hand

how much of

aperture

is

recal

ci

trance

aperture like preordained synchronicity

like overtures festooned in loam
like sonnets ferrying from the tongues of young tuatara

temporality smacks of the newly spilt & the already spoiling, of
surge & decay, delapidation & dentition

in case of fire make your way
to the nearest exit

the urge for extra innings is rampant
but rarely
forthcoming

aperture like indemnified alert

trampled between 2 mists   →   ruse arousal
cottonwood
a harlequin tripping over riptide

in the bilge of retribution, ... → lurk
a provisional bottom feeding cased in the throne of forgotten
obsequies

where in the wound is the pillage, the momentary *call-forth*,
the moment of execution

aperture approaches lattice during a heavy mist

froth furls the riverbed where a
boy & his dog are rafting

the query begins a conversation

which way the wind blows is
predicated upon heat

with aperture this melancholia

bruise bristling   ballistics
         non-calculability
a collapsing spirogyra
foams the red deserts

where in the lament is pullulation, the hobbling
that respires, the waltz loosed of metric, the scholastically
squamous, — tossed

with the undercoat newly glazed & cracking, → a
chill-leakage, a belled
serendipity,
lachromosity
jewelled with
unseasonable seizure

aperture balancing rigor mortis on a slippery incline

considers frugality flux   impermanence & throats of one
note   considers appreciating appreciation the stalwartness of
frog how little
commonality contributes to the common cause   conjures
disparity repaired by loft   uneasiness quieted by tribute
off to the side like some street urchin hatching from a vendor's
spatula
paint peelings summon to offer *stir* as a form of redecoration

undiluting the camphor of exigencies
the rill persists
quixotic & stricken

aperture achieves lull

commiseration
bleed-saddling

routinizations blunted the will subides
carry-overs on a tray of lisps

confessions careen in the milk of a lost ventriloquy

when wait is no longer contradictory
abatement becomes a loose form
of stepping

aperture risks

pinion   rack
     gear-rattle
tower-throttle
pelagic-rumbling

how much of
risk
is
willing-ness

measuring consequence while the grain resplendors in
perturbarance, in the wildly elemental

the shallows usurped by anecdote

the justices compromised

trembling, …
I place my head
         on
the wolf's paw

aperture disavows circumference

discolorings & constitutions

crests undulate rills   wheatfields   aspects

     cusps   underbellies   blush

"I am a werewolf," the man said.

"You don't look like a werewolf," the little girl replied.

"What do werewolves look like?"

"Scary."

forecasts stumble upon ordainment

honorariums stall

sequence initiates ceremonials with

werewolves

conspicuously absent

aperture approaches parentheses

aside from

in addition

a detour is an invitation to re-fasten

to elope to connubial eloquence

where in the willow-groves

are the sequester seeds

do songs

say it diffently

at the corner of Amsterdam & 81st

an old man plays the cigirtma

Listening

from afar

---

*Cigirtma (small fife) is a wind instrument made from the bone of an eagle's wing. It is mainly used by shepherds, and is today well on the way to disappearing. It has a total of seven holes, six on the top and one on the bottom, and is some 15–30 cm. long.

aperture allocates landscape

"Spread out before you is the landscape."

opening into/upon   entering

the other that extends   subsumes

consumes   enthralls/appalls   the "spread before"

that appears

the landscape plus what we bring to the landscape becomes our

point of

view   [departure points . . .

        wayfaring

        approximation assumes distance

        distance *teases* approximation

to view landscape in-itself, un-subjected, — is this possible?

can landscape view us?

Come the snow melt the brook blooms robust, burly, churls with

a contagious giddiness, a pony-glee-frolic

This is the disposition I assign it. Would the brook dispute this?

Language achieves landscape both combinatorially & singularly

"Melancholia" is a landscape.

"The lurch of gull-riddle rattling the thorax" is also a landscape.

where in the tear is *drift*

where in the toss does the appear
appear

coming into *beComing* that
which appears

becoming the
appearing

aperture envisions apparition

aris(ings)e   scaffold   rouse

r   i   n   s   e

rill

rustle

rupture

the outgrowth summoned   a beckoning   febrility
increases likelihood establishes lurk as both destination &
approach

which side of the street you are on *matters*

what kind of a rebuke is carnage? deniability is imbecility.   the
Eurasian war horse was a magnificent brute. the crossbow
altered warfare. as did the Colt multishot revolver.

the such of her arms
an embrace
continuously firing

aperture

this

just this

HELLER LEVINSON's previous books include *from stone this running, Smelling Mary, ToxiCity: Poems of the Coconut Vulva, Because You Wanted A Wedding Ring,* and *Another Line.* Levinson originated Hinge Theory which he envisions as Multiplicitous Exfoliations of Extensionality and Complementarity. His artistic and musical collaborations using Hinge Theory are growing rapidly and widely, as its applications are limitless. Levinson's poems and writings have appeared in hundreds of journals and literary outlets around the world. He lives in New York where he studies animal behavior. See more at www.hellerlevinson.com.

TITLES FROM BLACK WIDOW PRESS
TRANSLATION SERIES

A Life of Poems, Poems of a Life
by Anna de Noailles. Translated by Norman R.
Shapiro. Introduction by Catherine Perry.

Approximate Man and Other Writings
by Tristan Tzara. Translated and edited
by Mary Ann Caws.

Art Poétique by Guillevic.
Translated by Maureen Smith.

The Big Game by Benjamin Péret. Translated
with an introduction by Marilyn Kallet.

Boris Vian Invents Boris Vian:
A Boris Vian Reader.
Edited and translated by Julia Older.

Capital of Pain by Paul Eluard.
Translated by Mary Ann Caws,
Patricia Terry, and Nancy Kline.

Chanson Dada: Selected Poems by
Tristan Tzara. Translated with an
introduction and essay by Lee Harwood.

Essential Poems and Writings of
Joyce Mansour: A Bilingual Anthology.
Translated with an introduction
by Serge Gavronsky.

Essential Poems and Prose of Jules Laforgue.
Translated and edited by Patricia Terry.

Essential Poems and Writings of
Robert Desnos: A Bilingual Anthology.
Edited with an introduction and essay
by Mary Ann Caws.

EyeSeas (Les Ziaux) by Raymond Queneau.
Translated with an introduction by Daniela
Hurezanu and Stephen Kessler.

Fables in a Modern Key by Pierre Coran.
Edited and translated by Norman R. Shapiro.
Full-color illustrations by Olga Pastuchiv.

Forbidden Pleasures: New Selected Poems
[1924–1949] by Luis Cernuda.
Translated by Stephen Kessler.

Furor and Mystery & Other Writings
by René Char. Edited and translated
by Mary Ann Caws and Nancy Kline.

Guarding the Air:
Selected Poems of Gunnar Harding.
Translated and edited by Roger Greenwald.

The Inventor of Love & Other Writings
by Gherasim Luca. Translated by Julian &
Laura Semilian. Introduction by Andrei
Codrescu. Essay by Petre Răileanu.

Jules Supervielle: Selected Prose and Poetry.
Translated by Nancy Kline and Patricia Terry.

La Fontaine's Bawdy
by Jean de La Fontaine. Translated with an
introduction by Norman R. Shapiro.

Last Love Poems of Paul Eluard.
Translated with an introduction by
Marilyn Kallet.

Love, Poetry (L'amour la poésie)
by Paul Eluard. Translated with an essay
by Stuart Kendall.

Pierre Reverdy: Poems, Early to Late.
Translated by Mary Ann Caws and
Patricia Terry.

Poems of André Breton: A Bilingual Anthology.
Translated with essays by Jean-Pierre Cauvin
and Mary Ann Caws.

Poems of A.O. Barnabooth
by Valéry Larbaud. Translated by
Ron Padgett and Bill Zavatsky.

Poems of Consummation
by Vicente Aleixandre.
Translated by Stephen Kessler.

Préversities: A Jacques Prévert Sampler.
Translated and edited by Norman R. Shapiro.

The Sea and Other Poems by Guillevic.
Translated by Patricia Terry. Introduction by
Monique Chefdor.

To Speak, to Tell You? Poems by Sabine Sicaud.
Translated by Norman R. Shapiro. Intro-
duction and notes by Odile Ayral-Clause.

Forthcoming Translations

Earthlight (Claire de Terre) by André Breton.
Translated by Bill Zavatsky and Zack Rogrow.
(New and revised edition.)

The Gentle Genius of Cécile Périn:
Selected Poems (1906–1956).
Edited and translated by Norman R. Shapiro.

MODERN POETRY SERIES

WWW.BLACKWIDOWPRESS.COM